B8110

THE

THE BEACH
John Hodge

Adapted from the novel
by Alex Garland

faber and faber

First published in 2000
by Faber and Faber Limited
3 Queen Square London WC1N 3AU
Published in the United States by Faber and Faber, Inc.,
an affiliate of Farrar, Straus and Giroux, New York

Photoset by Parker Typesetting Service, Leicester
Printed in England by Mackays of Chatham PLC, Chatham, Kent

A CIP record for this book
is available from the British Library

ISBN 0–571–20486–4

2 4 6 8 10 9 7 5 3 1

CONTENTS

INTRODUCTION

by John Hodge

About a year after the release of *Trainspotting,* Andrew
Macdonald, Danny Boyle and I set about making our next film.
The Flop was filmed in Utah in the United States. It was known in
some countries as *A Life Less Ordinary* but in most places the title
was translated literally, becoming variously *Le Flop/Das Floppen/Il
Floppo/ The Big Flop* (USA)/*The Whopping Floperoo* (Aus. and NZ)
and in Japan it was *The Great Loss of Face.* The film, a story of love
and kidnap, provided an excellent backdrop for our publicity tour,
and there were even suggestions that it should be released for
viewing in its own right, although I am not sure if this ever actually
happened. *The Flop* was widely reviewed, attracting diverse and
heated opinion: 'a disaster' wrote one critic, 'a mess' wrote
another, and 'a load of rubbish' wrote yet another. It seemed (as
usual!) that those pesky critics just could not agree. But we
couldn't rest on our laurels for ever. We all knew that sooner or
later we would have to get off our big fat backsides, step forth and
make another motion picture.

We had intended to return to Utah but a few injudicious words
from one of our cast during a live interview on Radio Salt Lake
had put paid to that. If you were feeling generous you could blame
the root beer, but let's be honest, referring to the locals as
'polygamous Nazis' was asking for trouble. The actor in question
was air-freighted out amidst tight security and it seems unlikely
that Utah will ever again provide a Brit-friendly filming
environment.

We then read Alex Garland's novel, *The Beach*, and had one of
our Creative Discussions.

1ST FILM-MAKER

Well?

2ND FILM-MAKER

Yeah.

All right. I mean, why not?

OK, OK! No need to go on about it.

Decision made. So I started work on the screenplay, producing a series of scripts, each more compressed than the last. To convert a novel of average length into a film of average length, cuts are unavoidable. We all mourn the loss of our favourite moment/scene/character, but I don't believe there is any other way. On the same principle, it is important to discard from the successive drafts anything confusing or unnecessary. The only casualty that I really regret inflicting during this process was the loss of two plucky blokes from the north of England who, in one draft, turn up on the island with a camcorder to make a video diary for a BBC holiday programme. They're not in the novel, they had no right to be in the script, they were a pointless indulgence, I know. But I liked them. I fought for their survival, but to no avail. They never even made it to the re-write, poor souls, sent back to the vault, frozen for ever in their plucky blokiness. I can't even remember their names.

When the time came to cast the lead in the film, we considered many actors but elected to approach Leonardo DiCaprio, whom you may remember as the floating corpse at the end of that film about the sinking boat. Young DiCaprio had become quite a star following this heart-rending scene and we were most taken with his acting. We sent him a copy of the novel, the script and our most recent work, with its box-office figures tagged on to tantalize him still further. He was so impressed that he got in touch immediately after only six months had elapsed to say that he was going to make *American Psycho* instead so tough luck you English schmucks, you losers, you sad forgotten colonialists, you representatives of a nation in decline, you cultural yesterdays, you jerks. And so on. This may look to the casual observer like a negative response. But we are not so easily deterred. We decided to take it as a clear 'yes, please' and to proceed on that basis. The film business is founded on illusion and no one means what they say. In fact, no one even knows what they secretly mean behind what they say because to commit yourself to a meaning would risk being wrong, which is the unspeakable offence. So (follow me closely), if you insist forcefully enough that you do know what they secretly mean, you may just be able to convince all of Hollywood that no means yes. And insist we forcefully did.

After several more months of Beverly Hills high-jinks, dollar inflation, brinkmanship, and the limitless consumption of jet fuel, a deal was done and production on *The Beach* began in Thailand. What follows is the production script, including scenes that were subsequently cut from the finished film. Unfortunately, I am unable to retrieve the two northern blokes from my computer's deepest memory, that corner of a faraway disk where stuff goes when you delete the deleted items. But I think of them still, nameless though they may be. They lived for a day, exotic insects, and now they sleep, side by side, electronically dreaming of a sequel.

The Beach

INT. AIRPORT IMMIGRATION BOOTH. DAY

('Above title' credits during this scene.)

Close-up: a piece of shiny metal machinery moves up and down with a neat 'chunk' sound.

It is the passport stamp of an Immigration Official as he stamps a series of passports and hands them back to their owners.

He is an impassive Thai in military uniform. His head barely moves as his gaze shifts from each passport to its owner; his manner at once cursory and careful.

The passports are from all over the world. We barely see their assorted owners; just glimpses of arm or leg, sandals, duty-free bags, briefcases, suit, shoes, etc.

He takes an American passport. It is fresh and barely used; its many pages contain only one stamp, that of the Philippines.

The Official selects a blank page. He places the stamp over it. His hand hovers. He flicks back to the photograph.

The photograph is that of a young man.

The Official looks up to compare.

The young man is seen for the first time: early twenties, T-shirt, shorts and sandals. This is Richard. He returns the Official's stare and smiles.

                              RICHARD
         Hi there.

The Official's palm slaps down the stamp with a loud 'chunk'.

                                        CUT TO:

MAIN TITLE CREDIT: THE BEACH

3

EXT. BANGKOK. NIGHT

Richard, a large rucksack on his back, stands at the side of a busy junction in the centre of Bangkok while traffic buzzes past him: taxis, trucks, cars, motorbikes and 'tuk-tuks' – the motorized tricycles.

RICHARD
(*voice-over*)

Now, if you're looking for someone to blame, you could start off with my girlfriend. Ex-girlfriend, that is. You see, it was her idea. She's like: 'Let's go see the world together.' We got as far as the Philippines before we discovered that we didn't like being 'together'. She said that I wasn't enjoying myself enough. More than that, she said that I appeared to enjoy not enjoying myself. And of course, she was right. 'But isn't that the purpose of travelling?' I said. 'Experience, pleasant or unpleasant, it doesn't matter.' 'You're on your own,' she replied. So she takes off for Australia, and me – I'm looking at the next cheap flight out of Manila which turns out to be headed for Bangkok.

A tuk-tuk draws to a halt beside him. The Driver, a sharply dressed young Thai, gets off immediately and approaches Richard.

DRIVER

You want a hotel? No problem. I take you to the Khao San Road. Lots of hotels. Very cheap.

RICHARD

How much to get there?

The Driver then removes Richard's pack from his back while he talks and loads it on to the back seat of the tuk-tuk.

DRIVER

Khao San Road? No problem. I say one twenty baht – you say no! Sixty! I say one hundred – you say eighty – I say OK, you say OK – we both very happy.

Having loaded the rucksack, he turns around to face Richard again. He is holding a high-power water pistol which he offers to Richard.

But you got to ride shotgun.

4

RICHARD

What?

DRIVER

Sungkran. Thai New Year.

RICHARD

So?

DRIVER

We celebrate with water.

He holds out the pistol again. Richard takes it.

The sound of an approaching tuk-tuk grows louder.

RICHARD

With water?

The Driver ducks.

Richard is soaked by a bucketful of water that passes over the Driver.

The Driver stands up, dry.

The other tuk-tuk drives away. On it are two Thais, both laughing, one holding the empty bucket.

Water drips down Richard's face.

(*to himself*)

Celebrate with water.

EXT. BANGKOK. NIGHT

The single headlamp of the tuk-tuk shines out directly and brightly.

Extreme noise and light.

In the back of the tuk-tuk, Richard sits poised with the water pistol, leaning forward so that he and the Driver can shout their conversation.

DRIVER

You come to Thailand before?

RICHARD

No.

                    DRIVER
You like it?

                    RICHARD
So far.

                    DRIVER
You are from America? Not so many Americans here.
Australians, French, English: many English.

Richard sits back.

                    RICHARD
Yeah, well, nowhere's perfect.

                    DRIVER
Look! Quick!

*Another tuk-tuk is approaching from the side. In the back is a Thai
armed with a water pistol.*

Richard swivels and shoots, scoring a direct hit.

He and the Driver cheer.

*Richard sits back again, pleased with himself, just in time to be
drenched by a bucketful of water from the other side.*

EXT. KHAO SAN ROAD. NIGHT

*The tuk-tuk is stationary. Richard, soaking wet, hands over one
hundred baht and the water pistol to the Driver who is still bone dry.*

                    DRIVER
Thank you.

                    RICHARD
Yeah, nice working with you.

*Richard picks up his pack and starts walking down the street, picking
his way through the crowd of Thais and travellers.*

*A few waterfights are in progress. Once or twice he pauses to avoid a jet
of water that passes in front of him.*

He absorbs the scene as he passes boarding houses and hotels, and the

*shops and stalls selling food, clothes, pirated tapes, jewellery, travel
tickets and international phone calls. Restaurants are filled with
Western travellers watching American films or European sport.*

*Outside one shop a Travel Agent makes his pitch beside a board studded
with photographs of Thailand's tourist attractions.*

TRAVEL AGENT

Nakhon – Pathom – Phra Ptahom Chedi – Damnoen Sadual
floating market – eight hundred baht. Kanchanburi – Erwan
National Park Phrathat Cave, Huang Khamin Falls – six
hundred baht. Nam Tok, Hellfire Pass, Three Pagodas, Sai
Yok National Park – fifteen hundred baht.

Richard studies the board briefly but continues on his way.

RICHARD

(*voice-over*)

The Khao San Road. It's a decompression chamber between
East and West. You can make plans here for the rest of your
trip, or pack up your memories before you go home.

*Richard walks along the road. He is approached by a young male Thai
Hustler who walks backwards in front of him while making his pitch.*

HUSTLER

You need somewhere to stay?

RICHARD

I'll find somewhere, thanks.

Richard politely ignores each of his subsequent offers.

HUSTLER

What do you want? Sell your passport? Buy passport? Airline
tickets? You want silk? I'll take you to the best silk place? You
get a suit in twenty-four hours. Diamonds? You want to come
with me, you get present for your girlfriend. Maybe no
girlfriend? You want a girl, no problem. Good time. Boy-girl
fucking no problem. You want to drink some snake blood?

At this last one Richard stops and addresses the Hustler.

RICHARD

Did you say snake blood?

HUSTLER

Yes.

RICHARD

No thank you.

Richard turns away again. The Hustler picks up the pace behind him.

HUSTLER

What is wrong with snake blood?

RICHARD

I don't like the idea.

HUSTLER

May be you are afraid. Afraid of something new.

RICHARD

No, I just don't like the idea.

HUSTLER

Like every tourist, you want it all to be safe – just like
America.

Richard stops dead and turns to face the Hustler.

RICHARD

On the other hand.

INT. WINDOWLESS ROOM. NIGHT

*Richard gulps down a tall tumbler full of snake blood. He is watched by
the Hustler and two other Thai men. The room is bare apart from a
table on which stands a glass tank full of writhing snakes.*

RICHARD

(*voice-over*)

The genuine traveller, you see, will never decline a challenge.
To do so would be an act of heresy.

*Richard completes his drink. He licks his lips and studies the empty glass
like a connoisseur. He puts it down beside the tank of snakes and pulls
on his pack.*

Gentlemen: that was excellent.

The Thai men smile appreciatively.

INT. RESTAURANT. NIGHT

The restaurant extends deeply back away from the street. Richard passes many diners not dissimilar to himself. Some are talking, many are engrossed in the Hollywood film that is showing on a video-player.

At the back he reaches a reception desk where he drops his pack.

A female Thai Hotel Receptionist stands behind the desk. Two of her friends sit behind her.

RECEPTIONIST

Good evening.

RICHARD

Good evening. Do you have a room?

She shows Richard a 'menu' of available rooms. The menu offers a spread of prices for single/double/window/fan/air-con/bathroom.

Richard points to the cheapest combination.

I'll take one of those, thanks.

He hands over the requisite amount of baht from his wallet while the Receptionist takes care of some administration, copying out his passport number, etc.

Richard becomes aware that he is being stared at. He turns to look.

A man is standing at the bar a few yards away, holding a bottle of beer while he stares at Richard. This is Daffy: mid-thirties, gaunt and haggard.

Richard returns the stare briefly before he is interrupted by the Receptionist.

RECEPTIONIST

Your key.

She places it on the counter.

As Richard turns to pick it up, the Receptionist squirts at his face with a small water pistol.

Welcome to Thailand.

The Receptionist and her friends laugh at him as the water drips off his face.

RICHARD

Thank you.

INT. RICHARD'S HOTEL ROOM. NIGHT

Richard drops his rucksack to the floor and inspects the small spartan room.

There is a small window in the one solid wall. The other three are made of warped hardboard with half a metre of wire mesh at the top.

He pulls a cord and the fan turns slowly.

He opens a cupboard. Empty.

He looks under the bed. No rodents. A few roaches.

He sits on the bed. The springs are noisy.

INT. HOTEL CORRIDOR. NIGHT

The sound of the shower can be heard through a door marked with a shower sign.

The sound stops and the door is opened. Richard emerges with a towel wrapped around his waist, carrying his key and washbag.

He walks the short distance to his room. He puts the key in the door but the lock is stiff and he has to fiddle with it, bent over and dripping water on the floor.

While he is doing so, the sound of footsteps climbing nearby stairs can be heard.

There is the sound of a loud wolf-whistle.

Richard turns to the source of the whistle, removing his key from the lock.

A beautiful European woman is smiling at him. This is Françoise. She approaches and takes the key from his hand.

It is not clear what she is going to do with it or with him. Richard drops his washbag and his toiletries spill on to the floor. They stand for a moment alone in the corridor.

Françoise turns abruptly to the door. She inserts the key and turns it first in one direction, then the other, while twisting the handle.

FRANÇOISE
Et voilà.

The door swings gently open. She hands the key to Richard and stands back.

RICHARD
Thank you.

Footsteps approach from the stairs.

Françoise is joined by a young man, Etienne, who catches up with her. He nods at Richard as he takes her arm. They walk away from Richard to the next door.

FRANÇOISE
Bonsoir.

RICHARD
Eh – *bonsoir.*

ETIENNE
Goodnight.

The couple reach their door. They enter their room and the door is closed behind them.

Alone in the corridor again, Richard contemplates their presence.

RICHARD
(*voice-over*)
I was reminded, as if I needed to be, that I was alone because no one wanted to be with me.

INT. RESTAURANT. NIGHT

Richard is at a table eating some noodles and drinking a beer. On a high shelf several feet away a Vietnam War action movie – all gunshots, car chases and explosions – plays on the television.

Some other single travellers sit watching the film, but at the table next to Richard are three young travellers. Their dialogue fades in and out and is heard incompletely.

Richard's attention switches back and forth between the mindless film and his neighbours' conversation.

> RICHARD
> (*voice-over*)
> Now, the problem is this: everyone wants the experience – everyone wants to go somewhere new, do something different. The net result: everyone goes to the same places and everyone does the same thing.

> TRAVELLER 1
> So where did you just come from?

> TRAVELLER 2
> We went trekking. Chiang Mai. It was OK; we saw the hill tribes and stuff.

> TRAVELLER 1
> You smoke the opium?

> TRAVELLER 2
> Yeah, but it was like it was all arranged. There was nothing spontaneous.

> TRAVELLER 3
> Was it expensive?

> TRAVELLER 2
> Not bad. You have to haggle. Be prepared to walk away.

> TRAVELLER 1
> We're going to Ko Pha Ngan.

> TRAVELLER 2
> Yeah? I heard they had a sewage problem there.

I didn't know that.

TRAVELLER I

We were thinking of getting a flight to Saigon. Apparently Vietnam is really cool, like Thailand used to be.

TRAVELLER 2

Yeah, I always wanted to go there too.

RICHARD
(*voice-over*)

Vietnam. Why not? Why shouldn't it be the next destination. So much to offer – the great South-east Asian shorthand for suffering and the white man's adventure. Vietnam: the defining event of history for my generation. That is to say, that it defined us because we didn't know the first fucking thing about it. And I openly include myself in that. We couldn't tell you where it was, how long it lasted, what happened there or even what it was all about, but, hey – at least we'd seen the movie!

On the video screen, a yellow petroleum explosion fills the screen.

INT. RICHARD'S HOTEL ROOM. NIGHT

Some light enters from the street through a small window.

Richard lies on his bed, watching the fan rotate above him.

He is listening to the sound of Etienne and Françoise engaging in noisy sex in the room next door. They too have noisy bed-springs. They shout out in French and call each other's names as they reach the climax of their activity and then fall silent.

Richard relaxes with them.

Suddenly there is a disturbance from the room on the other side. A door slams and then a man's voice, Daffy's, starts shouting at the world.

DAFFY
(*off-screen*)

Everybody happy! Everybody having a good time! You know what we are?

There are a few shouts of 'shut-up' from other rooms but Daffy ignores them.

Richard lies in silence, listening.

DAFFY

Parasites! Viruses! Cancers! That's us, boys and girls. A big chunky charlie that's eating up the whole fucking world. And if it looks different, then no problem! Just pay them in dollars and fuck their daughters and turn it into Disneyland! It's beautiful! It's perfect! So kill it! Eat it up and shit it out!

He pauses for a moment. It seems that he may have finished.

Richard relaxes a little but is immediately startled by Daffy thumping furiously on the wall.

Hey!

Richard freezes and listens.

He hears nothing for a moment. Then another three loud thumps.

Hey, you!

Richard is momentarily terrified. With each thump the whole room seems to shake.

Another pause, then a face appears at the wire above Richard's head, one hand pulling at the mesh. It is Daffy.

Have you got anything to smoke?

Richard is momentarily shocked then leaps up to stand on his bed face-to-face with Daffy across the wire.

RICHARD

No! No, I don't have anything to smoke.

Daffy smiles as he replies in a loud whisper.

DAFFY

No problem, pal, 'cause I've got fuckin' loads of the stuff.

Daffy's other hand appears, holding a large joint, unlit. He fumbles in his pockets for a lighter.

It's supposed to help me sleep. I've been trying to sleep for months, but it won't work, it won't work, it won't fucking work. You know what I'm talking about?

Richard nods, noncommittal.

RICHARD

Yeah.

DAFFY

You've no fucking idea.

RICHARD

No, you're right, I don't.

Daffy lights the joint, draws deeply and exhales. He relaxes.

DAFFY

Ah! That's better.

He offers the joint through the mesh to Richard, who takes it.

RICHARD

Thanks.

Daffy closes right up to the wire.

DAFFY

It was the beach, you understand. The beach: too beautiful, too much input, too much sensation. So I try to keep it under control, but it just keeps spilling out!

RICHARD

Right.

DAFFY

You see, the beach is on an island. The island is perfect. I mean real perfection. I don't mean just nice. The real fucking thing, OK? Perfect. A lagoon. Sealed in by cliffs. You could sail right past it, you'd never know it was there. Totally fucking secret, totally fucking forbidden. No one can go there. But a few people went, once upon a time. Not your usual travelling fools, you understand. Men and women with ideals. Do you believe in that place?

RICHARD

Nope, but I'd guess you're going to tell me I should.

DAFFY

It doesn't matter what I say any more. It's up to you. Ideals, we had. Huh! We were all just parasites. The big chunky charlie. I was trying to find the cure. I said leave! Leave this place! But they wouldn't listen. So if they want you, they can have you. I don't care any more. It's up to you.

RICHARD

You know what, no offence and all, but you're fucked in the head, right?

For a moment it is not clear how Daffy will take this.

His face becomes impassive and stern. Then a smile spreads across his lips.

Abruptly Daffy sticks his hand crashing through the wire mesh towards Richard and he speaks without whispering.

DAFFY

Richard. It's been nice knowing you!

Richard smiles politely. They shake hands.

RICHARD

Yeah. Sure. You too.

INT./EXT. RESTAURANT. DAY

The restaurant fronts on to the street where a new day's activity is beginning.

Richard watches this as he eats his breakfast.

He notices Etienne and Françoise sit down at the next table.

RICHARD

Bonjour.

ETIENNE

Good morning.

FRANÇOISE

Did you sleep well?

RICHARD

Not too bad.

FRANÇOISE

I hope the noise did not keep you awake.

Richard looks from one to the other.

RICHARD

The noise? Don't worry. You're on holiday.

ETIENNE

She means your neighbour. The Scotsman.

RICHARD

Oh, that noise! Yes, he certainly did.

ETIENNE

We moved rooms because of him.

FRANÇOISE

He tried to borrow money from us. He said if we lent him money he would tell us about a secret beach.

ETIENNE

On an island that no one can get to.

FRANÇOISE

But he has been there, of course.

ETIENNE

It was ridiculous: all this at three o'clock in the morning.

RICHARD

It would be nice though, if there was a place like that. You know, that no one could get to.

ETIENNE

Of course, but look: all these people. If that place existed, they'd all be there.

INT. RESTAURANT/GUEST HOUSE. DAY

Richard is concentrating intensely as he plays a two-person video fighting game (e.g. Streetfighter*). He has a Walkman, the earphones draped around his neck.*

RICHARD

(*voice-over*)

He was right: we'd all be there, turning it into somewhere that we could get a burger and play video games. You couldn't stop that process any more than you could stop yourself breathing. And pretty soon, there won't be anywhere left to go.

Richard's game character is killed.

'Game Over' flashes on to the screen.

INT. HOTEL STAIRWAY/HOTEL CORRIDOR. DAY

Richard climbs the stairs, a tape playing on his Walkman.

On the landing a Thai woman is cleaning the floors, wall and ceiling with a mop and bucket of water. In the course of this she has spread a lot of water.

Richard stops and looks on aghast as she mops around a naked light bulb.

RICHARD

Be careful. Electricity.

He mimes an electric shock.

She continues her work.

THAI WOMAN

Chill man. No worry.

Richard edges past her and along the corridor, attempting to stay off the wet areas of the floor.

She calls to him.

Hey – there is a letter for you!

RICHARD

What?

THAI WOMAN

A letter. For you.

Richard walks towards his room.

On his door, a folded sheet of paper is attached with a pin.

Richard lifts it off and unfolds it.

It is a detailed and carefully drawn map of a cluster of islands. Some are named. One is unnamed. On it, some features are marked: hills, forest, river and a letter X.

In the corner it reads 'X = beach'.

Richard switches off his Walkman.

He studies the map then walks to Daffy's door and knocks.

No reply.

Richard twists the handle and pushes gently. The door opens.

INT. DAFFY'S ROOM. DAY

The room is dim, but even so the blood can be seen sprayed and smeared around the walls, sheets and floor.

There is no sign of Daffy.

Richard treads carefully, avoiding the pools of blood on the floor.

He reaches the other side of the room. There, wedged in the narrow gap between bed and wall, is Daffy's corpse. His wrists have been cut.

Richard studies the map again.

RICHARD
(*voice-over*)

You hope and you dream, but you never believe that something's going to happen for you, not like it does in the movies. And when it does, you sort of expect it to feel different. More visceral. More real. Like IMAX, maybe. I was waiting for it to hit me, but it just wouldn't come.

Richard switches his Walkman back on.

INT. HOTEL ROOM. DAY

In a different room in the hotel, two Policemen, one in uniform sits with a typewriter and the other, a Detective, stand over Richard while he signs a statement.

> ### RICHARD
> (*voice-over*)
> The police didn't want to waste any time on it. They were just pissed because he was travelling on a false passport.

> ### DETECTIVE
> Name of Mr Daffy Duck, birthplace Neverneverland. Kind of fucks up all the paper work.

> ### RICHARD
> (*voice-over*)
> They pulled everyone in from the hotel but they didn't want much.

> ### DETECTIVE
> You sign the statement. It says he cut his wrists: already dead when you found him.

> RICHARD
> (*voice-over*)
> And they didn't ask about a map, so –
> (*on-screen*)
> No problem.
> (*voice-over*)
> I didn't tell them.

Richard signs.

The Detective studies Richard's passport.

> DETECTIVE
> What are you doing in Thailand? Tourist?

> RICHARD
> Traveller.

> DETECTIVE
> You go to Patpong? See smoke from pussy; ping-pong ball from pussy; razor blade from pussy; bird from pussy.

> RICHARD
> I don't think so.

> DETECTIVE
> Why not? Thai girls best in the world. Thai food best in the world. Thai dope best in the world.

> RICHARD
> I wouldn't know anything about that, sir.

INT. HOTEL CORRIDOR. DAY

The door of the room opens and Richard walks out.

Lined up in the corridor, slouching against the walls, are several other travellers from the hotel. At the front of the queue are Françoise and Etienne.

The Officer beckons Etienne into the room and closes the door.

Richard and Françoise acknowledge each other with a smile.

INT. RICHARD'S HOTEL ROOM. DAY

Richard is seated at the top of his bed, addressing his speech out of shot while he holds the map.

RICHARD

OK, this island may not actually exist. And even if it does, we might not be able to get there. But look at it like this: what else is there to do around here?

He rethinks for a moment.

I just wondered if you'd like to come with me.

We see that Richard is alone.

So what do you think? Are you going to come or not? I'd be thrilled if you'd join me, you and your . . . you and your boyfriend.

INT. HOTEL CORRIDOR. DAY

Richard knocks on his neighbours' door.

Etienne opens it.

RICHARD

Hi. You want to take a hike? I mean a trip. A journey. With your girlfriend and me? I mean the two of you, and me. It's the secret island. Paradise. You know the kind of thing I'm talking about.

Françoise appears behind Etienne.

Richard pauses and begins again, more composed. He holds up the map so that they can both see.

Everybody want to do something different, but everyone does the same thing.

Françoise takes the map from him and studies it. Richard watches.

RICHARD
(*voice-over*)

I realized that I had absolutely no idea of how I was going to get there.

EXT. KHAO SAN ROAD. DAY

Françoise and Richard watch through the window of a shop while Etienne inside haggles forcefully with the Thai Travel Agent.

> RICHARD
> (*voice-over*)
> But Etienne – and I have to hand it to the guy – was great.

EXT. RAILWAY/THAI COUNTRYSIDE. NIGHT

A train travels at night alongside fields.

> RICHARD
> (*voice-over*)
> He organized the whole thing: tickets, timetables, the whole damn trip.

INT. TRAIN. NIGHT

Richard is awake. Opposite him, Etienne and Françoise are slumped together in sleep.

EXT. SEA. DAY

The bow of a passenger ferry crashes through a wave.

EXT. BOAT. DAY

The decks are crowded with travellers and their packs. Among them are Richard, Françoise and Etienne. Maps and guidebooks are being studied by many. The noise of the engines and the wind deters conversation.

> RICHARD
> (*voice-over*)
> Thanks to him, we hit the final stop on the tourist trail inside twenty-four hours, where, Etienne assured me, we would hire what he called a 'local fisherman' to take us on the last stage of our journey.

INT./EXT. TRUCK. DAY

Inside the back of a covered, converted pick-up are eight people – four people are seated down each side, among them Richard, Françoise and Etienne.

Behind them, as they bump along, can be seen the dusty red road bordered by dense green shrubs.

The truck stops.

EXT. ROAD. DAY

Richard unloads the last of the three rucksacks from the roof of the truck, passing it down to Etienne who stands at the back with Françoise.

The truck pulls away, revealing a sign: 'Seashell Bungalows'.

EXT. BUNGALOW. DAY

A simple wooden shack on stilts; one of several standing in a line at the edge of the beach. There is a small porch to the front.

INT. BUNGALOW. DAY

A spartan room: bed, mosquito nets, chair.

Richard dumps his rucksack.

EXT. SEA/BEACH. DAY

A long inflatable tube is towed past by a motorboat, its passengers whooping with delight.

As it passes, Françoise is revealed, standing in the water, looking in towards the shore. She begins to walk in.

On the beach there are sunbathers, games of beach volley ball, and vendors selling food and sunglasses.

RICHARD
(*voice-over*)
This was just the kind of place I didn't want to hang around.
Not that it's lacking in comfort. Quite the opposite. It's got

everything. Everything you could possibly need to make you feel at home. And what's the point of that?

On the beach Françoise picks up a towel.

EXT. BEACH RESTAURANT. DAY

The restaurant fronts on to the beach. At the back there is a bar.

Richard sits alone at a table with a drink, watching the scene on the beach, including Françoise.

Etienne pulls up a chair and sits down.

Françoise will join them as the dialogue proceeds.

                    ETIENNE
It's arranged. Tomorrow morning. Eight hundred baht.

                    RICHARD
Nice work.

                    ETIENNE
There is one problem.

Etienne opens the map on the table.

He will not take us to the island. It's in the National Park and it is forbidden to go there. But we are allowed to travel to this one to stay for one night.

                    RICHARD
That's the wrong one.

                    ETIENNE
I know that.

Françoise sits down with a drink.

                    RICHARD
So from there to there?

                    FRANÇOISE
We swim.

RICHARD

Swim?

FRANÇOISE

We leave our rucksacks on this island and then we swim.

ETIENNE

You can swim?

RICHARD

Yes, of course I can swim.

ETIENNE

So no problem.

RICHARD

And how far do you think it is?

ETIENNE

One or two kilometres.

RICHARD

Great. Not far at all.

He picks up the map.

ETIENNE

It will be worth it, Richard. An adventure: and just the three of us.

EXT. BUNGALOWS. EVENING

In heavy rain, Richard walks among the bungalows towards his own. He reaches the door during his rant.

RICHARD

'Just the three of us.' 'Just the three of us.' 'Can you swim?' 'I can swim. And I have a beautiful girlfriend.'

He stands at his door.

Shit!

He kicks the door. He curses and kicks it again a few times.

On the porch of the bungalow next door are seated two men. They are

Zeph and Sammy, Americans in their early twenties. They have a few bottles of beer and some snack food.

They watch Richard impassively.

Richard ceases his assault on the door.

Sammy addresses Richard, who replies tersely.

> SAMMY

Locked out, huh?

> RICHARD

Yeah.

> SAMMY

Lost your key?

> RICHARD

Yeah.

> SAMMY

Bummer.

> RICHARD

Yeah.

Pause.

> SAMMY

Do you want a beer?

EXT. BUNGALOW. NIGHT

All three are stoned. A joint is passed around, and beer bottles are drunk from. They swat half-heartedly at mosquitoes.

> SAMMY

So it was a kind of thrilla in Manila?

> RICHARD

That's right.

> SAMMY

You give up your job, you borrow from your old man, you sell your car. And –

(snaps fingers)

– she takes off.

                    ZEPH

Sammy, the guy probably doesn't want to talk about it.

                    SAMMY

Nothing like travel to test a relationship.

                    ZEPH

Jesus.

                    SAMMY

You're probably better off without her.

                    ZEPH

Sammy, how the fuck would you know if he's better off
without her or not? You never even met her.

                    SAMMY

Just trying to comfort the guy, through the dark times.

                    RICHARD

Don't worry, it's not a problem.

                    SAMMY

You see, Zeph – it's not a problem.

ZEPH

Sammy, change the fuckin' subject.

SAMMY

OK, OK, I know. I'll tell him the story of the KMF.

ZEPH

KFM.

SAMMY

Zeph, if you're going to get picky about this – you can tell
him.

Zeph exhales a long cloud of smoke before he speaks.

ZEPH

I presume that you know the story of the Kentucky-fried
mouse?

RICHARD

Woman bites a chicken leg: turns out to be a mouse. It's an
urban myth.

ZEPH

Exactly. Always happened to a friend of a friend of someone
else.

RICHARD

So?

ZEPH

So there's an urban myth, well, more of a rural myth, going
around here at the moment. It's about a beach.

RICHARD

Uh-huh.

ZEPH

Yeah. This beach is perfect. It's on an island, right, hidden
from the sea. Imagine: pure white sand and enough dope to
smoke all day every day for the rest of your life. Only a few
know exactly where it is and they keep it absolutely secret. Of
course, no one's actually ever met any of these people, only
met someone who has. You know what I mean?

SAMMY

It's a Kentucky-fried mouse.

ZEPH

Although I must say, if I had the key to a place like that, I'd keep it to myself. You don't want every asshole in Thailand turning up.

SAMMY

What do you think, Richard? You heard that one before?

RICHARD

I hadn't but it's good. It's a good story.

A torch shines on them, jolting them into some sort of reaction and a woman's voice calls out.

RECEPTIONIST

Hey, you! I got your key!

INT. BUNGALOW. DAY

Richard's rucksack is packed and by the door.

Richard is sitting copying Daffy's map on to another sheet of paper.

RICHARD
(*voice-over*)

Now I made a decision. I don't say it was the best decision I ever made.

EXT. BUNGALOW. DAY

Richard kneels on the porch of Zeph and Sammy's bungalow, beside the empty bottles and other debris.

RICHARD
(*voice-over*)

But, at the time, it seemed reasonable to me. I told myself that it was an act of comradeship, but if you were being critical you'd say that I was just like everybody else, shit-scared of the great unknown, desperate to take a little piece of home with me.

He slips the folded copy under their door.

He looks around to check that he has not been seen.

EXT./INT. TRUCK. DAY

Richard, Françoise and Etienne, their packs on their backs, are walking through and away from the bungalow compound towards a passenger truck that stands idle on the road, awaiting its passengers.

> RICHARD
>
> Hey, listen, I was wondering: what would you think if we met some other people and they seemed like they were OK – you know, good people – what would you think?

> ETIENNE
>
> What?

> RICHARD
>
> Of taking them with us?

> ETIENNE
>
> Richard, it's secret. The map, the island: secret.

> RICHARD
>
> Yeah. I'm not saying we should tell everyone.

> ETIENNE
>
> It would be a big mistake to tell anyone.

> FRANÇOISE
>
> Have you told someone?

> RICHARD
>
> No, of course not.

They have reached the truck.

> ETIENNE
>
> It's a secret, Richard, that's the whole point.

Etienne throws his pack on to the top of the truck.

> RICHARD
>
> Right.

(*voice-over*)
And that was it. We didn't talk about it any more. We were on our way.

EXT. BEACH. DAY

Richard walks along a narrow wooden pontoon, his rucksack on his back.

Etienne and Françoise follow.

He stops about half-way along at a small narrow wooden boat with an outboard motor.

He looks down into it.

RICHARD
(*voice-over*)
So it turns out that local fisherman don't actually exist any more. You want fish? Put down dynamite. You want to go somewhere –

Etienne and Françoise walk past him along the pontoon without stopping and disappear from view.

– get a taxi.

EXT. SEA. DAY

Richard, Françoise and Etienne sit at the back of a small powerful motor-launch which skims across the surface of the sea with great noise and speed.

EXT. BEACH. DAY

The motor-launch idles gently as it drifts into the shallows of a small deserted bay.

Richard, Françoise and Etienne jump from the boat into the shallows.

EXT. BEACH. SUNSET

As the sun sets, they sit in silence, each shovelling down forkloads of noodles.

EXT. BEACH. NIGHT

The only sounds are those of crickets and the waves gently breaking on the shore.

Richard is lying asleep on the sand.

He is woken by someone rummaging through the rucksack beside him. It is Françoise, removing clothes, books, souvenirs. Eventually she finds her camera, a mini-tripod and a cable-release.

She places them on an unfolded T-shirt on the sand.

> RICHARD

Françoise –

> FRANÇOISE

Shh. Etienne will be angry if I wake him. He thinks I waste film taking photographs of the sky.

Richard wakes up and works out what she is doing.

> RICHARD

I think so, too.

> FRANÇOISE

One night I will get the perfect photograph.

She presses the cable release.

> *Un, deux, trois, quatre, cinq, six.*

She lets the shutter close.

> Take a look.

Richard leans over and squints down the viewfinder.

The sky is framed. Françoise leans into the frame.

Richard draws back.

RICHARD
You realize that in the eternity of space, there is a planet, just like this one, where you are photographing back towards us. You're photographing yourself.

FRANÇOISE
Incredible.

RICHARD
There are infinite worlds out there, where anything that can happen, does happen.

FRANÇOISE
So, on one you are rich, on another poor. On one a murderer, on another the victim.

RICHARD
Exactly.

FRANÇOISE
Richard, you know something –

She hands him the cable-release while she adjusts the camera.

– that is just the kind of pretentious bullshit that Americans always say to French girls so that they can sleep with them.

RICHARD
Sorry. I thought I was doing quite well.

FRANÇOISE
It's just the sky, Richard.

She presses his thumb down on the cable-release, her hand around his.

Un, deux, trois, quatre, cinq, six, sept . . .

EXT. NIGHT. SKY

Françoise's voice fades away over an image of the night sky.

Time lapse: the sky rapidly changes to day.

> RICHARD
> (*voice-over*)

When you develop an infatuation for someone, you always find a reason to believe that this is exactly the person for you. It doesn't need to be a good reason, a bad one will do just as well. Taking photographs of the night sky, for example; in the long run that's just the kind of dumb, irritating habit that would cause you to split up. But in the haze of infatuation – it's just what you've been searching for all these years.

EXT. BEACH. DAY

From a different beach they look towards their target: the island. It is one or two kilometres away.

Richard, Etienne and Françoise stand on the beach looking towards it.

Each is in their swimwear and a T-shirt, and carries a plastic bag, inflated and tied, in which they carry their valuables and some rations.

> ETIENNE

One kilometre.

> FRANÇOISE

Two.

> ETIENNE

Richard?

> RICHARD

I don't know – I'm American.

> ETIENNE

So?

RICHARD

We think in miles, not kilometres.

ETIENNE

So how many miles do you think it is?

RICHARD

I have no idea, but it looks like a long way. If it's too far, then we'll drown. But if we don't try, then we'll never know.

Richard wades into the water.

So: let's go.

(*voice-over*)

I am such a fucking hero: 'Let's go.' I felt like I'd waited all my life just to say something like that. So I replayed it a couple of times, taking it from different perspectives.

EXT. BEACH. DAY

Multiple repeats of Richard's moment from various perspectives and speeds.

RICHARD

So: let's go.

(*voice-over*)

You have to enjoy a moment like that. You just don't know, you see; it may never happen again.

Once more.

RICHARD

So: let's go.

He dives in and begins swimming.

EXT. SEA. DAY

They are far out to sea now, several hundred metres from the shore.

Richard swims at the front, the other two about five metres behind.

RICHARD

Everyone OK?

ETIENNE

We're OK.

RICHARD

I think we're about half-way.

A few strokes later.

ETIENNE

Richard – I saw a fin!

RICHARD

What!

ETIENNE

A fin!

They all stop and tread water.

RICHARD

A shark fin?

ETIENNE

I don't know: just a fin. Over there. About a hundred metres.

RICHARD

Big?

ETIENNE

Yes.

RICHARD

Well, what the fuck do you expect me to do about it?

ETIENNE

Nothing, I just thought you ought to know.

RICHARD

Well, to be honest, Etienne, I would rather have not known about it.

ETIENNE

I'm sorry.

RICHARD

A bit fucking late.

He starts swimming again.

A few strokes later he hears a short sharp scream from Françoise.

ETIENNE
Françoise! Françoise!

Richard turns around. Françoise is gone. Her plastic bag bobs on the surface. Etienne is frantic, hysterical.

She is gone!

RICHARD
What happened?

Etienne submerges briefly and resurfaces.

ETIENNE
She just went under the water. She was pulled under. Oh God, I don't see her.

RICHARD
Was there a shark? Did you see a shark?

They both start looking down at their feet and circling frantically in the water.

ETIENNE
I don't know! I don't know! Oh God.

Suddenly Richard screams.

Françoise surfaces, pulling up his ankle.

She and Etienne laugh at Richard.

RICHARD
Very funny. You Europeans, you have such a playful sense of humour. No wonder your comedy has conquered the world.

He swims on.

ETIENNE
What about Molière?

RICHARD
Fuck off.

He swims on without looking round.

EXT. BEACH. DAY

One by one the three swimmers emerge from the sea and collapse on the beach. They are absolutely exhausted and lie there on the sand, unable to speak.

Eventually, they tear open their plastic bags, drink some water and eat some chocolate.

Richard has a little water left in his bottle. He notices Françoise and Etienne eyeing it enviously.

He holds the bottle out towards them, then snatches it back and swigs down the last of the water.

EXT. FOREST. DAY

Richard, Françoise and Etienne walk through the forest behind the beach.

EXT. FOREST. DAY – LATER

They scramble up a steep slope through dense foliage.

Richard, at the front, pauses to let the other two pass him, then he follows.

EXT. TOP OF SLOPE/CLEARING. DAY

Richard reaches the top of the slope and follows the other two through a gap in the foliage.

He joins Etienne and Françoise who are standing in awe at the edge of a large clearing filled with cannabis plants.

ETIENNE

Now this is what I call a lot of dope.

They smile and examine the plants.

Richard wanders a short distance away.

He sees a monkey sitting on the branch of a tree at about head-height. He approaches it slowly.

The monkey sits still. Richard feeds it his last piece of chocolate.

He smiles, then suddenly notices that the monkey has a thin rope around its neck. The rope trails down to the ground.

Richard is alarmed to see where the rope ends: tied to the wrist of a man sleeping in the long grass. He is a Thai, a cannabis Farmer. A Kalashnikov rifle lies by his side. His physique is strong and his skin weathered.

Richard turns back to look at Etienne and Françoise. They are still strolling amongst the plants.

Richard begins to back away.

The monkey jumps from the branch, excited.

The rope tightens.

The Farmer wakes.

He lifts his gun and stands up to look out over the dope field.

EXT. FIELD. DAY

There is no one there.

EXT. AMONG PLANTS. DAY

In a line, Richard, Françoise and Etienne crawl along the earth beneath the cannabis plants. They are tense and frightened.

EXT. FIELD. DAY

The Farmer looks around, sees nobody. His attention is attracted by a whistle.

He looks over. A group of three similarly armed Farmers emerge from the forest at the other side.

He waves at them. They beckon to him.

He sets off through the field.

EXT. AMONG PLANTS. DAY

The three intruders continue to crawl along the ground between the plants.

Suddenly Richard stops. The Farmer's footsteps come closer.

His feet pass in the gap between Richard and Françoise. He pauses. They lie frozen in place. He lights a cigarette and drops the match. He moves on.

They breathe again.

EXT. FOREST. DAY

Richard, Françoise and Etienne run uphill through less dense forest.

EXT. HILLTOP. DAY

Sweating and out of breath, they reach the top of the hill. They stop.

Beneath them in one direction is the field and forest through which they fled.

Beneath them in the other direction is the beautiful lagoon surrounded by cliffs.

> FRANÇOISE
> My God, what are we doing?

ETIENNE
Shit. That was not on the map, Richard.

RICHARD
I didn't draw the map, Etienne.

ETIENNE
It's a fucking mess.

RICHARD
I didn't force you to come, so don't blame me.

FRANÇOISE
We should get off this island.

RICHARD
Get off this island? How? Swim? Great idea. Back in the water? Well, fuck that. You swim back if you want to. Both of you. But over there, somewhere – I think – is paradise.

ETIENNE
Richard – she is frightened. So am I.

Richard looks at them. They await his lead.

RICHARD
Well, we're not going back.

Richard smiles. The other two are still nervous.

(*voice-over*)
Once again, I think you'll agree: a moment worth savouring.

EXT. FOREST. DAY

They are travelling downhill now, beside a stream.

RICHARD
(*voice-over*)
The most satisfying aspect, of course, was that Monseigneur Practical, he turned out to be not so hot in your actual primordial fight or flight situation, your combat zone. I didn't need to say anything. I knew it; he knew it; and so did she.

They stop to drink from the stream.

44

If we follow this down, it should lead us all the way.

Françoise and Etienne say nothing.

(*voice-over*)
So I was feeling pretty pleased with myself. I was in full command of the situation.

EXT. WATERFALL. DAY

Water thunders from a cliff-top to a pool.

Richard, Etienne and Françoise lie on a flat rock at the edge of this high waterfall. It falls in a single giant step.

On either side of the waterfall, cliffs curve away to form a massive circle enclosing the lagoon and an area of land covered in forest.

Etienne turns to Richard. Françoise continues to look down as she drops a stone and watches it arc into the pool below.

>ETIENNE

Well?

>RICHARD

Well what?

ETIENNE

How do we get down?

RICHARD

How do we get down? How am I supposed to know? Jesus!
Do I have to decide everything now?

FRANÇOISE

We'll jump.

The men ignore her.

ETIENNE

You wanted to be in command, Richard.

RICHARD

I only took command because you lost your nerve, French
Boy.

ETIENNE

And look where you have taken us.

FRANÇOISE

We'll jump.

They ignore her again.

RICHARD

Etienne, if you're not happy with the way things are going,
OK, you take over, sir!

Richard salutes.

ETIENNE

We'll climb down there.

He indicates to the side of the waterfall.

FRANÇOISE

We can jump.

RICHARD

Françoise, we're not going to jump, so just can it, OK? And
climb down that cliff? That is an asshole suggestion.

ETIENNE

You're calling me an asshole?

RICHARD

Yes, I am, and that's just the start.

ETIENNE

All right, fuckface, let's do it!

He shoves Richard. They square up for a fight.

FRANÇOISE
(*shouting*)

Please!

They turn to her. She is standing with her back to the drop.

RICHARD

No!

SLOW-MOTION:

Richard and Etienne rush towards her to try to restrain her as she turns and jumps.

Their hands snatch at the air just as her feet leave the rock.

NORMAL SPEED:

She falls towards and into the pool.

Richard and Etienne scramble to the edge and peer over.

She surfaces and waves.

Richard and Etienne look at each other.

OK, so: we'll jump.

EXT. WATERFALL. DAY

Richard and Etienne jump.

They sink and then surface.

All three are ecstatic and elated, charged with the excitement of the fall and the joy of journey's end. They exchange hugs and kisses.

They become aware of a single person clapping slowly.

They turn to see Keaty, a young Afro-Caribbean Londoner, standing a few paces away.

KEATY

Congratulations. It took me the best part of an hour to work up the balls to do that. Mind you, I was on my own, so you have to make allowances.

They say nothing.

I think maybe you'd better meet Sal.

INT. LONGHOUSE. DAY

Sal, a woman in her early thirties, is seated on the floor opposite Richard, Françoise and Etienne.

Sal is studying Daffy's map. She hands it back to Richard.

Gathered around them are about twenty assorted inhabitants of various nationalities, all weathered travellers in their twenties or thirties.

The longhouse is a single-storey building made from wood and bamboo lattice, about thirty metres long. It is divided up by low partitions into single or double sleeping areas, some of which are personalized, others not. In the centre of the building is a thick wooden post on which are carved indications of the passing years: 0000, 0001, 0002, etc. There is also an open area where this action takes place.

RICHARD
(*voice-over*)

At first they were more interested in the map than us.
(*on-screen*)

The guy who drew it –

SAL

Daffy?

RICHARD

Yeah. He's dead. Cut his wrists open in a hotel room on the Khao San Road.

Sal is serious; but does not seem surprised or upset. She looks directly at Richard.

> SAL

Well, that's sad news. He was one of the founders of our community. But he became depressed.

> RICHARD

The police didn't know what to do with the body. I guess they'll incinerate him or something.

> SAL

Do you think he gave a map to anyone else?

> RICHARD

I don't think so.

> SAL

And you, have you shown anyone this map?

> ETIENNE

No.

> FRANÇOISE

No.

RICHARD

No.

SAL

Good. We value our secrecy.

Sal produces a cigarette-lighter and sets the map alight. It burns.

EXT. GARDEN/CLEARING/LONGHOUSE. DAY

Richard, Etienne and Françoise follow Keaty through the lush gardens and into the clearing towards the longhouse. As they walk they are watched by all the inhabitants of the community.

RICHARD
(*voice-over*)

Now I've got to say that my first impressions were not one hundred per cent favourable. Oh God, I thought, it's a tribe of hippies.

EXT. ISLAND SCENES. DAY/NIGHT

Commence a montage of various scenes of island life involving its citizens and the newcomers.

The longhouse stands at one edge of a clearing, dominating it. Scattered around are several other smaller huts and a few tents. Other locations are the beach, the garden, and the forest.

We see the inhabitants:
– at work in the garden
– in the lagoon
– relaxing on the beach
– around the fire at night.

RICHARD
(*voice-over*)

I thought we'd have to talk about our positive energies a lot, kiss the earth every morning and recycle our waste products by some unspeakable mechanism. Fortunately not. It really was some kind of a paradise.

EXT. FOREST/BEACH. DAY

*Tracking through the darkness and enclosure of the forest to emerge
suddenly on to the light and space of the beach which is now revealed in
all its glory.*

EXT. GARDEN. DAY

Sal addresses them as she walks through the garden.

> SAL
> OK, this is the garden. Some of us work here, some of us go
> fishing, some cook, and some build. Even paradise takes a
> little shaping.

INT. LONGHOUSE. DAY

*Everyone, including Françoise, Etienne and Richard, is sitting around a
big wooden table set for dinner. Two people are serving side dishes of
vegetables and rice.*

> SAL
> And we grow our own, OK? That means you don't steal from
> the farmers on the other side.

> ETIENNE
> They know that we are living here?

> BUGS
> Oh, yeah. But they keep to their side and we don't trespass on
> their turf.

> SAL
> A couple of years back, they came to us, they said: we can
> stay, but no more, no more people. Which kind of suits us,
> too.

> KEATY
> So you were lucky.

> FRANÇOISE
> It was Richard, he saw them before they saw us.

                           SAL
Clever Richard.

                         RICHARD
                       (*voice-over*)
Sal was the leader but it wasn't a big deal. There wasn't any
ideology or shit like that, it was just a beach resort for people
who don't like beach resorts.

*One man begins drumming softly on the table with his hands. Another
joins in, then another. Soon everyone is tapping out a rhythm, against
the table or a bottle or a coconut shell, using their hands or a knife or
chopsticks.*

*This is intercut with the following scenes to the point where the
newcomers have joined in and it reaches a crescendo as the main dish –
a magnificent platter of fish and fruit – is served.*

EXT. ISLAND SCENES. DAY

*Various characters are introduced in different locations; at work or at
rest; speaking to Richard or (as if to him) to camera.*

First the three Swedes.

                         RICHARD
                       (*voice-over*)
There were the Swedes: Christo, Sten and Karl.

                         CHRISTO
We like fishing.

                           KARL
Fishing. Yeah.

                           STEN
Yeah.

                         CHRISTO
And in the winter we like skiing.

                           KARL
Yeah.

                        STEN
Yeah.

                        CHRISTO
But in Thailand – there is no skiing.

They seem momentarily sad.

                        RICHARD
                       (*voice-over*)
There was Keaty, who only cared about two things.

EXT. BEACH. DAY

*Keaty stands alone at the wicket of a cricket pitch on the sand delivering
a sermon, echoing off the cliffs, to no one. He holds a bat and ball.*

                        KEATY
We thank you, Lord, for the twin pillars of civilization,
Christianity and cricket – even when played by those of
another faith.

He tosses the ball up and hits it for six.

EXT. ISLAND SCENES. DAY

                        RICHARD
                       (*voice-over*)
Then there were the Yugoslavian girls.

                        SONJA
We are from Sarajevo.

                        MIRJANA
Our hearts are full of loss.

                        RICHARD
I'm sorry.

They start laughing at him.

                        SONJA
It's all right.

> **MIRJANA**

We tell everyone that.

> **RICHARD**
> (*voice-over*)

There was Weathergirl.

> **WEATHERGIRL**

I feel a tightness in my pelvis; it's gonna rain.

Heavy rain falls.

*On the beach, Etienne sits between an Australian man and woman –
Rod and Sandi.*

> **RICHARD**
> (*voice-over*)

Rod and Sandi were Australian, so of course they were the
only people on the beach who couldn't speak English.

> **ROD**

The kid's on for young and old – like he gets in a bingie,
hoicks a gibber at the dickless Tracy.

Etienne has not a clue, but is too polite to say.

> **ETIENNE**

Right.

> **SANDI**

Fellow's a crow-eater, so what do you expect?

> **ETIENNE**

Of course.

EXT. CLEARING. DAY

*A man, Unhygenix, is gutting and chopping a pile of fish, up to his
elbows in blood and guts.*

> **RICHARD**
> (*voice-over*)

Our resident chef was known as Unhygenix.

EXT. SHOWERS. DAY

Unhygenix stands under the shower, scrubbing his arms vigorously with soap and brush.

> RICHARD
> (*voice-over*)
> On account of his obsession with soap.

Unhygenix places the soap on a ledge beside a pile of different soaps. He picks up one of these and tries it instead, then another, and another but none seems to work.

> UNHYGENIX
> Fish! Fish! Fish! Still I smell of fish. Always fish!

EXT. CLEARING. DAY

Richard is playing with a Gameboy.

> RICHARD
> (*voice-over*)
> There was a range of sporting and leisure activities to suit all tastes.

He struggles but loses. He looks up. Across the clearing he sees Ramone smiling at him sympathetically.

Ramone signs to Richard.

> RAMONE
> (*signing*)

Game over.

Nearby, Andy translates.

> ANDY

Game over.

EXT. CLEARING. DAY

> RICHARD
> (*voice-over*)
> And although it's true that, yes, there was a man with a guitar.

> GUITARMAN
> (*singing badly*)
> 'Come as you are, as you were, and as I want you to be . . .'

> RICHARD
> (*voice-over*)
> They were actually a pretty good bunch of people.

EXT. BEACH. DAY

On the beach, Keaty is now arranging the entire community in the fielding positions of a cricket game while batsmen wait at two sets of makeshift stumps.

> KEATY
> Wicket-keeper! Slip! Slip! Gully! Silly mid-off! Short leg! Square leg! Deep square leg! Fine leg! Deep cover! Right arm over the wicket, three balls remaining. Is there anybody who does not understand?

One person raises a hand tentatively. Then another, and another, until everyone has raised a hand.

EXT. CLEARING. DAY

Bugs is working on the roof of the longhouse.

> RICHARD
> (*voice-over*)
> The only person I didn't like was Sal's boyfriend, Bugs.

> BUGS
> Can you do this, Richard? Could you make a chair? A man should have a talent in his hands.

> RICHARD
> (*voice-over*)
> He was one of those pricks who just won't shut up about all the great things they've seen and done.

EXT. CLEARING. NIGHT

At night, Bugs addresses a small group of people around the fire.

BUGS

We were in the desert for three weeks. It's forty-eight in the shade and there's bugger all of that to speak of. We're on one and a half litres of water a day: it's practically suicide. But every morning we'd look east and see the sunrise, and I'd think, if I die today – it's worth it.

Bugs looks distant and thoughtful.

There is a general rolling of eyes.

INT. LONGHOUSE. DAY

The drumming reaches its crescendo and the fish and fruit platter is laid out to cheers.

INT. LONGHOUSE. NIGHT

Richard and nearly everyone else is lying on their bed. Joints are being smoked and a few candles burn.

Sonja is standing up. She addresses everyone.

SONJA

OK: 'Tomorrow I will travel for many miles on a bicycle to visit my aunt who herds goats in the mountains.'

She points at Keaty.

Keaty repeats the phrase but in Serbo-Croat.

One by one, as Sonja points, the others repeat the phrase in Serbo-Croat.

RICHARD
(*voice-over*)

This became our world and these people our family. Nothing else mattered. Back home was just one more place we didn't think about. I settled in –

It is Richard's turn. He repeats the phrase.

I found my vocation.

EXT. BEACH. DAY

Richard is standing in waist-deep water. He is holding a bamboo spear.

Beside him are Etienne and Françoise, similarly armed.

Their hair is longer and their tans deeper than when they arrived.

They are watching Christo, who stands a short distance away, spear poised for the kill while he talks through the process.

> CHRISTO
>
> OK. Now you stand still. You wait. The fish come. And then –

He suddenly throws the spear into the water. He lifts it out, triumphant.

> You kill.

A dying fish wriggles on the end of the spear.

> Now, you try.

Richard, Etienne and Françoise wade apart a little and into deeper water. They wait and look.

EXT. UNDERWATER. DAY./EXT. LAGOON. DAY

Their feet and legs are visible. At first, nothing is happening, then a few fish swim into view.

Richard throws and misses. The other two throw and miss.

CHRISTO
No, no, no. Too fast. Slowly.

They pause.

Richard throws. He hauls his spear from the water and holds it aloft, a fish wriggling on the end.

RICHARD
Yo! And I say unto you: I shall provide!

EXT. CLEARING. DAY

A bamboo spear, loaded with fish like a giant kebab, is carried across the clearing towards the cooking area where the Chef and his helpers are at work.

The spear is held by Richard who smiles as he deposits the fish on the broad wooden chopping surface.

INT. LONGHOUSE. DAY

Richard is talking to Keaty who lies on his bed reading Wisden (*an anthology of cricketing statistics*).

RICHARD
Hey, Keaty, did you hear the news? I've got an aptitude, a hidden talent. I'm an old-fashioned hunter-gatherer.

KEATY
The Lord has smiled upon you.

RICHARD
He has?

KEATY
He has made you sharp of eye and swift of limb.

RICHARD

If I see him, I'll thank him.

Richard turns to leave.

KEATY

He'd appreciate that. And well done: first day's fishing, first day's catch. I'd say you lot are just about ready to join our community.

RICHARD

I thought we already had.

KEATY

Not yet baptized, my son, not yet baptized.

EXT. CLEARING. NIGHT

A blade burns in the fire.

Keaty lifts the knife from the fire.

The entire community is assembled, watching.

RICHARD
(*voice-over*)

Every community has its rituals. Ours was simple: last one to arrive tattoos the next.

He takes Etienne's wrist.

KEATY

It hurts. OK?

Etienne nods.

Keaty swiftly cuts the simple symbol just below Etienne's shoulder and smears blue powder into the cut.

Etienne winces.

Keaty finishes and hands the knife to Etienne who heats the blade briefly in the fire before he turns to Françoise. He kisses her arm before he cuts.

Françoise takes the knife.

Richard offers his arm. She grips it tightly. She hesitates.

He looks into her eyes.

She cuts. He grimaces. She works on, holding his arm.

INT. LONGHOUSE. NIGHT

A few candles still burn as people prepare to turn in for the night.

Richard is lying in his sleeping area. He is watching Françoise.

RICHARD
(*voice-over*)

So everything was working out pretty well, except for one thing. Desire is desire, wherever you go. The sun will not bleach it, nor the tide wash it away.

She is standing, visible only from the waist up above a partition. She is inspecting her tattoo.

A hand, Etienne's, appears from below, beckoning her down.

She takes the hand.

Just for a moment, her eyes meet Richard's, and then she lowers herself towards the ground, disappearing from view.

The last candle is extinguished.

EXT. BEACH. DAY

A game of soccer is in progress, involving most of the population, men and women.

Etienne is playing well.

A few people, not involved in the game, are scattered along the beach, relaxing. Among these are Françoise and Richard, who is watching the game.

RICHARD

He's good.

FRANÇOISE

Who?

RICHARD

Etienne. He's good at soccer.

FRANÇOISE

Oh. I wouldn't know.

RICHARD

You don't like soccer?

FRANÇOISE

No. It's so boring.

RICHARD

Yeah, but he is good. Look. Nearly scored.

FRANÇOISE

Is that good or bad?

RICHARD

I think it's good. Not that I think there's anything good about being good at soccer. All you've got to do is be naturally talented and practise a lot. Anyone could do that. I could do it if I wanted to, I just don't want to. That's all.

She sits up.

FRANÇOISE

Richard.

RICHARD

Yes?

FRANÇOISE

What are you talking about?

RICHARD

I don't know. Just conversation.

FRANÇOISE

Do you have a girlfriend?

RICHARD

Here?

FRANÇOISE

Anywhere.

RICHARD

No. Why?

FRANÇOISE

Just conversation.

RICHARD

I'm not jealous, if that's what you're thinking.

FRANÇOISE

No, it's what you are thinking. You are far from home. You meet a girl. It's exciting, why not? You are attracted to her – it's in your eyes. Perhaps in hers as well. So you think something might happen: it's easy to believe, you want it to be true. But she has a boyfriend, so you are jealous. Don't worry: it's natural. Now I have seen enough football. Shall we swim?

Richard is stunned.

RICHARD

So would I be wrong?

FRANÇOISE

What?

RICHARD

If I thought something might happen – would I be wrong?

She touches him.

FRANÇOISE

Richard, how would I know? I don't know any more than you.

She walks away.

Richard watches her go. He turns to the football.

Etienne scores.

RICHARD
(*voice-over*)

And that's all it takes. Nothing more than a few words and the softest touch and your life is different, won't ever be the same again. Man dies, leaves you the mystery map to the secret island: happens every day. But you get a smile from someone you want: well, that's special, that's worth the journey.

INT. LONGHOUSE. NIGHT

Richard is sitting on his bed.

He is watching Françoise in conversation with Etienne across the other side of the room. During Richard's voice-over their conversation ends and Etienne walks away, leaving Françoise momentarily alone.

Most of the population is present in the room. Sal is reading.

Without warning or invitation, Keaty sits down in front of Richard and begins talking to him.

KEATY

One: she's just teasing you.

RICHARD

What are you talking about?

KEATY

Two: you don't speak French. Three: he speaks French. In fact, better than that, four: he *is* French. Five: he's better at football – sorry, soccer – than you. Six: you're a bit strange, Richard. Some girls like that in a man but not usually the sort of girls you want to be with. Seven: you have a history of non-functional backslash dysfunctional relationships.

RICHARD

A what?

KEATY

Your last girlfriend chucked you. Must be a reason.

RICHARD

It wasn't my –

KEATY

And eight: you have well-developed thumbs.

RICHARD

What does that mean?

KEATY

You enjoy video games. A powerful index of incompatibility.

RICHARD

Keaty, why do I feel that you're trying to tell me something?

KEATY

You haven't got a hope, mate, not a bleeding chicken's chance in Thailand.

RICHARD

Thanks, Keaty.

KEATY

My pleasure.

He gets up and walks away.

Françoise is alone now. Richard watches her for a moment. She looks in his direction but seems to look right past him before the centre of the room is occupied by a commotion, obscuring his view.

At the heart of this are Bugs and an Italian man, Gregorio. Bugs is holding a pair of pliers. Gregorio is in pain.

Richard watches.

> BUGS

I can deal with it!

> GREGORIO

I don't want you to deal with it.

> BUGS

It won't take a minute.

> GREGORIO

No! Please, no! I must go to the mainland.

Onlookers join in.

> VARIOUS

No way/
You can't go to the mainland/
No, *etc.*

> GREGORIO

Sal!

Sal looks up for the first time.

> SAL

Sorry, I wasn't really tuned in. You want to go to the mainland? To see a dentist, is that it?

> GREGORIO

Yes.

Sal is casual but firm.

> SAL

No. It's out of the question.

She returns to the book.

With help from two or three other people, Bugs drags Gregorio to the floor and rips out the offending tooth with the pair of pliers. Gregorio screams.

Richard watches.

Sal appears beside him while they watch.

How's it going, Richard?

RICHARD

Fine.

SAL

You OK about this?

RICHARD

Yeah. I mean, we've got a secret here, right? We all have to be prepared to take a little pain to keep it that way.

SAL

Excellent. Excellent attitude.

She leaves him.

Gregorio screams as Bugs completes his work.

EXT. CLEARING. NIGHT

Gregorio's expression is glazed and he sways gently as Bugs raises another cup of fruit alcohol to his lips. His tooth is now on a string around his neck.

BUGS

There you go. Kill the pain, boy.

A short distance away, Richard watches this.

To his other side, a circle of about five people, including Etienne, are playing cards in animated fashion. There is no sign of Françoise.

RICHARD
(*voice-over*)

All things considered, I wondered whether Keaty was right, I never had a chance and even if I did, it had come and gone. Maybe, I thought, that day on the sand, that was it, that was as close as I would get to her.

FRANÇOISE
(*off-screen*)

Richard?

She is standing right over him.

RICHARD

Yes!

FRANÇOISE

Would you like to come to the beach with me?

Richard looks at her, then across at Etienne, still engrossed in the card game, then back to François.

RICHARD
(*voice-over*)

And at that moment realised that no, Keaty – he was the one who got it wrong.

EXT. BEACH. NIGHT

Richard and Françoise walk down the shore to the moonlit sea.

Françoise wades in up to her thighs. Richard follows.

FRANÇOISE

Are you happy, Richard?

RICHARD

Happy? Yes, I love being here. It's great.

FRANÇOISE

Do you think that I ignore you?

RICHARD

Me? No.

FRANÇOISE

But I do. It's because I am with Etienne. It's difficult for me to spend time with you.

RICHARD

I don't suppose there's any special reason that you should, spend time with me, that is.

FRANÇOISE

But of course there is: I like you, a lot.

RICHARD

And have you mentioned this to Etienne?

FRANÇOISE

No. It's our secret.

They are very close now, looking into each other's eyes.

Suddenly Françoise looks away.

There!

RICHARD

What?

FRANÇOISE

Look! The plankton. Shrimps. In the dark, when they are disturbed, they glow.

She dives in. He follows.

EXT. UNDERWATER. NIGHT

Their faces, close together, are illuminated by the phosphorescent plankton.

EXT. BEACH. NIGHT

They surface, kissing passionately.

They make love in the water.

INT. LONGHOUSE. DAY

Everyone is seated around the table eating a big lunch. Richard and Françoise are opposite but apparently ignoring each other.

RICHARD
(*voice-over*)

OK, so 'Everybody loves a lover': that's what they say, but we preferred not to put it to the test. We didn't want the world to know.

UNDER TABLE. DAY

Under the dinner table all the legs and feet are visible. Richard's and Françoise's are entwined.

EXT. FOREST. DAY

Richard is walking along a path. He reaches a bush at what seems like the end of the path. He looks around, as though expecting someone.

> RICHARD
> (*voice-over*)
> But you know how it is: one way or another –

He pushes the bush aside.

> – the world always finds out.

Ahead of Richard is a secluded pond in which Sonja, Mirjana and Weathergirl are bathing.

> (*on-screen*)
> Sorry, I was looking for someone else.

They giggle at Richard.

EXT. FOREST/GARDEN. DAY

A machete hacks into a piece of tree.

Richard and Etienne are at the edge of the cultivated area where the shrubs are encroaching back on to the garden.

They stand a few yards apart, both hacking at the growth with machetes. Etienne seems sullen and preoccupied.

Etienne pauses.

> ETIENNE
> I want to talk.

> RICHARD
> What about?

> ETIENNE
> You and Françoise.

Richard stops.

RICHARD

What do you mean, me and Françoise?

Etienne hacks violently at a plant. Richard stiffens.

ETIENNE

I mean, Richard –

He hacks again.

– that I want her to be happy!

RICHARD

Of course. Of course. We all do.

ETIENNE

Shut up, Richard – and if happy is with you, then I will not stand in her way.

RICHARD

Etienne, you've got the wrong idea.

ETIENNE

Fuck you, Richard: I know. Everybody knows.

They stand in silence for a moment.

Then Etienne begins hacking violently at the bushes again.

> RICHARD
> (*voice-over*)
> I couldn't blame the guy. He had every right to hate me. And
> he did.

INT. LONGHOUSE. NIGHT

Everyone, including Richard, is seated casually around the clearing.

Etienne stands up to address the various people around the fire.

> ETIENNE
> OK, everyone, can I make a short announcement.

He continues in French and Helen translates.

> ETIENNE
> (*in French*)
> I know what has happened, so you don't all need to talk
> behind my back any more. I'm sorry if you feel awkward. I
> don't. It's just an alteration in the domestic arrangements.

*Richard, sitting beside Françoise, is suddenly conscious of everyone's
attention.*

EXT. BEACH. DAY

A tropical lightning storm is in progress.

*At the edge of the beach, Christo, Sten and Karl are standing under the
ineffectual shelter of a palm tree, each holding their spear. A short
distance away, under another tree, sit Richard and Françoise.*

Etienne is sitting alone and isolated on the beach, half-way to the sea.

*They are all contemplating the sea and the sky. Christo has a swimming
mask and a snorkel.*

> CHRISTO
> The problem is seeing the fish. With the rain and the poor
> light, they are very difficult to catch. It could last for days.
> Sometimes when it rains, we get hungry.

Richard takes the mask and snorkel from Christo and marches down towards the sea.

In doing so he passes Etienne but they do not acknowledge each other.

Richard pulls the mask on and marches into the sea.

EXT. LAGOON UNDERWATER. DAY

Richard swims along near the seabed past rocks and coral but can see no fish.

He surfaces and swims further out.

He hears shouts from the shore. He turns and treads water.

The shouts from his colleagues are indistinct, carried away by the wind the rain.

> RICHARD
> (*shouting*)

I can't hear you.

He takes the mask off to clean the lens.

And you can't hear me.

He puts the mask back on and turns away from the shore.

He freezes.

He looks around. The shore seems far away. He starts swimming frantically towards it in a state of blind panic.

There is a shark's fin in the water, moving towards him.

The shark closes.

Richard submerges and turns to face the shark.

The shark approaches head on. It is about five feet long with the appropriate teeth.

Richard braces himself for an attack, his spear held out in front.

The shark swoops towards him at speed.

It is closing right on him. He is terrified.

INT. LONGHOUSE. NIGHT

Richard is telling his story.

> RICHARD
> The important things are one: remain calm, and two: show no fear.

EXT. LAGOON UNDERWATER. DAY

The shark stops, its teeth centimetres from his mask.

Richard is astonished.

The shark circles him and approaches again, pausing just in front.

Richard circles frantically trying to follow it.

> RICHARD
> (*voice-over*)
> Because sharks can sense fear and panic just as easily as they can sense blood.

The shark swoops towards him again, missing narrowly.

The shark circles.

75

INT. LONGHOUSE. NIGHT

Richard continues.

> ### RICHARD
> The next thing to remember is that you will only have one chance to kill. After that, it will kill you.

EXT. LAGOON UNDERWATER. DAY

Richard thrusts his spear at the shark several times, missing completely.

The shark does not react.

Richard gives up. The shark bobs in front of him.

> ### RICHARD
> (*voice-over to longhouse*)
> And so it went for me, just as I knew it would, as nature had ordained: its jaw wide open, row upon row of razor-sharp teeth glinting underwater like jagged diamonds, its tail fins sweeping back and forth as it surged in for the kill. My whole life flashed before me.

INT. LONGHOUSE. NIGHT

Grilled shark steaks have been passed around and eaten by all while Richard stands and relates his adventure. He glances at Françoise, who listens with pride.

> ### RICHARD
> I had nothing left to offer but pure reflex. Mankind's basic drive for survival that shouts: 'No! I will not die today!'

EXT. UNDERWATER. DAY

Continuing the shark scene.

The shark is bobbing in front of him, practically wagging its tail.

Richard is smiling.

> ### RICHARD
> (*voice-over to longhouse*)
> And at that instant, it was either the shark or me. The shark knew it, I knew it.

Richard's arms flex. The spear travels up. It stops. Richard grips the spear tightly as it shakes.

Blood spurts out towards Richard's mask in pulses and the sea turns red around him.

Nothing personal, of course. Just the way the world turns. And I swear that in the last flicker of its eyes there was a moment between us, when it said –

INT. LONGHOUSE. NIGHT

Richard continues his story.

RICHARD
'Hey, Richard – enjoy your dinner.'

There are cheers to the end of his story.

Bugs waits until these die down.

BUGS
Strange thing, killing a shark, isn't it?

RICHARD
Just a big fish, Bugs.

BUGS
Just a big fish? Maybe. Maybe when it's still a baby and it hasn't really learned to kill yet, then maybe it's just a big fish. But when it's a great white angry mother with the taste of human blood on its tongue, well, then it's a different story.

Richard yawns noisily. Some people laugh.

He notices Bugs scowling at him.

RICHARD
Sorry, Bugs. Is it just me or does this wet weather make everybody tired? Maybe we can hear your 'very different' and I'm sure 'very interesting' story some other time.

There is a flurry of exaggerated yawning, sniggering, extinguishing of candles and calls of 'Goodnight'.

77

Very interesting.

Keaty repeats this in Serbo-Croat. Soon everyone is saying 'very interesting' in a range of languages.

Bugs does not laugh. He stares at Richard.

Richard is smiling as he extinguishes the final candle, Françoise, at his side.

RICHARD
(*voice-over*)

For a while, we were untouchable in our happiness.

EXT. CLEARING. DAY

Under a shelter in the cooking area, the Chef walks up to two sacks of rice and slashes them open.

RICHARD
(*voice-over*)

And then one day, the rice went rotten, and after that, one way or another, so did everything else.

He picks out two clumps of green, rotten mush and holds them out towards Sal, who stands nearby.

EXT. CLEARING. DAY

The inhabitants of the community are sprawled around the area, generally facing towards Sal who addresses them. Françoise is sitting with Richard.

SAL

All right, I've got some bad news. As some of you may have heard, a couple of sacks of rice have got contaminated with a fungus. Now this is not a disaster –

VARIOUS

Oh, no.

SAL

Yeah, that's right: I need a volunteer to go to Ko Pha Ngan

with me to buy some rice. So please, don't all volunteer at once.

There are no volunteers. Everyone avoids Sal's eye.

Keaty?

KEATY
I went last time.

SAL
And so did I. Anyone else?

Still no volunteers.

Richard?

RICHARD
What?

SAL
What about you? Will you come to Ko Pha Ngan with me?

RICHARD
Me? Well, I don't know –

Bugs raises his arm.

BUGS
I'll come with you.

SAL
It's all right, Bugs; Richard's going to come with me, aren't you?

RICHARD
Am I?

SAL
Who thinks Richard ought to come with me?

All hands go up, except Bugs.

Richard sees that he has no choice. He smiles.

RICHARD
Sure. Yeah. I'll go to Ko Pha Ngan.

Great.

She smiles back at him.

INT. LONGHOUSE. DAY

Richard is sitting on his mat with a pencil and a piece of paper. A line of people wait to pass him some crumpled baht and their order.

Several people, including Sten and Christo, give Richard letters to post during the shopping requests.

Their recitals overlap and freely intercut.

CHRISTO
Toothbrush, toothpaste, sixty cigarettes, a new hat, some Elastoplast, a pair of swimming trunks, four bars of chocolate and some razors.

WEATHERGIRL
One hundred aspirin, one hundred paracetamol, six boxes of regular tampons, toothpaste, soap and some shampoo.

KARL
I want a bottle of vodka.

STEN
Toothpaste, a ball of string, four double-A batteries and twenty condoms. No, make it forty.

MIRJANA
Six bars of chocolate, moisturizer, four boxes of tampons – assorted sizes – two bars of soap and some toothpaste.

UNHYGENIX
It's mixed in with my genes now. Smell it; it's a part of me. I am becoming a fish. Ordinary soap is a waste of time, Richard: I need something toxic, something industrial.

GUITARMAN
One tin of beef curry.

SONJA
A newspaper, some boiled sweets, shampoo and conditioner,

two hundred cigarettes, a pair of plastic sandals – small – a
new swimsuit – size ten, bright but no flowers, a plain T-shirt
– a jar of Vegemite and three cigarette lighters.

COMMUNITY MEMBER
Not square. Not oval. In between. Like old-style but not
exactly. I don't want a tribute band, you know what I mean. I
want like sunglasses used to be before it all got so
commercialized. Now it's such a statement. This is me.
These are my glasses. All that crap. I don't want modern,
retro or classic. I certainly don't want post-modern. Maybe
post-post-modern. Neo-modern, OK – but only if you can't
get anything else.

KEATY
A copy of the *Daily Telegraph* and as many triple-A batteries
as you can carry.

SHERIDAN
Make me a happy woman, Richard: fill this bag with soft bog
roll, Tampax and mosquito repellant.

NINA
Six hundred two-inch nails and a ball of string.

JOSH
Anything based on sugar. Chewy sweets, hard sweets, boiled
sweets, chocolate, biscuits, cookies, fruit cake, a couple of
Danish pastries maybe, some Turkish Delight or a piece of
halva even. Halva, that would be really nice.

STACY
Cigarettes chocolate tampons batteries.

MYRIAM
Cumin, saffron, cinnamon, condom, tampon.

BINDU
Jasmine tea, tiger balm, hand cream, lip balm, tea tree oil,
bath oil, shampoo, hair conditioner, skin conditioner, toning
lotion, hand cream, liposomal skin cream, moisturizing
cream, deodorant, anti-perspirant and make-up remover.

GUNILLA

A nail file, a G-string and a book by Barbara Cartland.

The last to sit down opposite Richard is Bugs. He sits close, their knees almost touching.

Richard is poised with his pen, ready to take notes.

RICHARD

Anything I can do for you?

Bugs smiles.

His right arm whips out and he grabs Richard by the testicles.

Richard buckles forward in pain.

BUGS

Yeah. When you get to Ko Pha Ngan, keep your hands to yourself and your dick in your pants.

He releases Richard.

Perplexed and in pain Richard watches Bugs walk away.

INT. LONGHOUSE. NIGHT

Richard is sleeping.

INT. HOTEL CORRIDOR. DAY

Richard approaches Daffy's room in the Khao San Road hotel.

INT. DAFFY'S ROOM. DAY

Richard enters Daffy's room and finds the body as before.

He leans down to inspect the body.

Daffy's hand shoots out to grab Richard as Bugs did.

DAFFY

Pay them in dollars and fuck their daughters and turn it into Disneyland, Richard!

Richard is in agony.

INT. LONGHOUSE. NIGHT

Sal wakes Richard.

EXT. BEACH. DAWN

Sal and Richard are walking away from the longhouse in the early morning light. Sal has a small parcel of cannabis wrapped up in a plastic bag. Richard carries the letters and money, similarly wrapped.

> RICHARD
>
> Why are we leaving so early?

> SAL
>
> If you hang around, people take advantage of you, give you orders for all sorts of shit – clothes, condoms, Vegemite and God knows what else.

> RICHARD
>
> Right.

> SAL
>
> We go to Ko Pha Ngan, sell the dope, buy the rice, and come back. That's all.

EXT. BEACH/WATER. DAY

Sal walks into the water and begins swimming out towards the cliff.

Richard watches then dives into the water.

EXT. LAGOON/CLIFFS. DAY

Sal waits for Richard as he catches up with her at the base of the cliffs inside the lagoon.

> RICHARD
>
> Over?

> SAL
>
> Under.

> RICHARD
>
> Anything I should know?

SAL

Don't breathe in until you get to the other side.

Sal submerges.

Richard watches her disappear into an underwater tunnel into the rock.

He takes a deep breath.

EXT. UNDERWATER. DAY

Richard enters the tunnel, passing from the light into the dark.

He enters near total darkness.

Far ahead is a narrow point of dim light.

He swims towards it.

INT. CAVE. DAY

Richard surfaces, short of breath, spluttering and gasping. He is in a cave within the cliffs, from which a small entrance opens on to the sea beyond.

Within the cave is a large flat rock and moored beside that is a small narrow boat with an outboard motor.

The ceiling of the cave is high and opening into it is a chimney (which will be in use later). Additional light enters through this.

As Richard surfaces, Sal is already in the boat.

She watches patiently as he recovers.

SAL

Welcome to the garage.

RICHARD

I think I nearly drowned.

SAL

Don't worry, Richard: that which does not destroy us makes us stronger.

She pulls the start cord. The small engine's loud roar reverberates around the stone walls.

EXT. SEA/CLIFFS. DAY

The small boat emerges from the cave on to the sea; Richard at the front and Sal at the helm.

EXT. SEA. DAY

Richard is at the front of the boat, watching the water glide past beneath the prow.

Sal is at the back, steering.

Richard glances back. He sees the island receding behind her.

He turns to face her.

> RICHARD

Sal!

She slows the engine until it idles. They drift.

> SAL

What?

> RICHARD

It's an awkward subject.

> SAL

Oh good, I love awkward subjects.

> RICHARD

Maybe not this one. Back on the island, no one talks about it.

> SAL

Well, you're off the island now.

> RICHARD

Exactly. Like Daffy.

> SAL

What?

> RICHARD

Well, that's it, isn't it? You see, I found his body. I think I have a right to ask about him.

He was depressed. He didn't like the longhouse. For him it
was a step too far.

RICHARD

He wanted everyone to leave?

SAL

Yeah: 'Let it return to nature.'

RICHARD

So why did he give me the map?

Sal laughs.

SAL

Richard, I have no idea. Maybe he liked you. Maybe he
hoped you would lead us off his promised land. I don't know.
Maybe for no reason other than he was fucking crazy. He held
an extreme view. Taken to its logical conclusion, I'd say
suicide was his only option.

She pauses for a moment.

But you're right: it's an awkward subject.

*She revs the engine. They move. Richard looks at the island once more
then turns to the front of the boat again.*

RICHARD
(*voice-over*)

No reason other than he was plain fucking crazy. I wasn't so
sure about that. But she was right about the suicide; it was his
only option. Because if you don't like paradise, where else is
there to go?

EXT. BEACH. SUNSET

*At sunset they come to land on a deserted stretch of beach. Richard
jumps into the shallows as Sal cuts the engine.*

Lights dance in the sky some distance away.

Sal and Richard drag and shove the boat up the beach.

The full moon shines brightly. The insistent beat of dance music is heard.

> RICHARD
> (*voice-over*)
> I'd been sort of looking forward to air-conditioning and some cold beer, but when we got to Ko Pha Ngan –

EXT. BEACH RESORT. NIGHT

The street is lined with bars, each pumping out Western music on its own sound system while Western tourists drink and party. One of them is being sick down a side-alley. Overweight Western men talk to Thai girls. Young men in football shirts inspect the goods at a stall selling handcuffs, switchblades and coshes.

Richard and Sal walk along the strip.

They turn towards a bungalow complex. Sal is still carrying the parcel of dope.

> RICHARD
> (*voice-over*)
> – I just wanted to leave again. In one moment I understood more clearly than ever why we kept the secret. Because if we didn't, then sooner or later, they'd turn it into this.

EXT. BUNGALOW RECEPTION. NIGHT

The reception area is covered by an awning. An old warped pool table stands in the centre. Sal and the receptionist, Sumet, greet each other and speak in Thai.

> SAL
> Good evening.

> SUMET
> Good evening, how are you?

> SAL
> Very well, thank you.

> SUMET
> You brought something?

SAL

As always.

Sal puts the parcel on the desk. Sumet weighs it in her hand.

SUMET

Good.

INT. PHONE BOOTH. NIGHT

*Richard is in one of a line of booths in an international call office/
general tourist store.*

RICHARD

I don't know. I just don't know. Maybe this year, maybe not.
I like it here. Things are different out here.
(*voice-over*)
I phoned home and discovered that I couldn't communicate.
I realized that I was no longer the person they knew.
(*on-screen*)
Yeah. Yeah. Sure, of course. Yeah, I'll call again. I promise.
Sure. Goodbye.

He hangs up and turns away.

Goodbye.

*He steps out of the booth. On the other side of the store are racks of
patterned shirts and hats.*

Richard walks across and stares just beyond them.

He is looking in a mirror, at himself, tanned and weather-beaten.

INT. SUPERMARKET. NIGHT

*Richard browses, selecting the items on his list, including a pair of
sunglasses chosen at random from a rack.*

In addition to these, he picks up a disposable camera.

RICHARD
(*voice-over*)
In fact, the more I thought about it the more I realized that
none of this world made any sense to me. I'd left it behind

and I would have been happier if everyone else could have done the same, but they weren't ready yet: they still needed that fix from home.

EXT. STREET. NIGHT

Richard studies the various letters that he has been given to post, their addresses spanning the globe.

> RICHARD
> (*voice-over*)
> To me it was clear, the more contact we had with the outside world, the more we would be corrupted and the sooner we would be discovered. The only way to survive was to cut ourselves free.

He tears up the letters and drops and scatters them across a muddy puddle.

EXT. BEACH. NIGHT

The music is far away now. Richard and Sal struggle along the deserted beach to their boat carrying a pallet laden with sacks of rice.

They arrive and drop the pallet.

EXT. BAR AREA. NIGHT

Richard and Sal walk along the strip of bars.

While they are walking and talking, they pass one bar outside which are seated Zeph, Sammy and two German women, Hilda and Eva.

Zeph notices Richard across the other side of the street and attracts Sammy's attention.

> SAL
> So how does it feel to be back in the world?

> RICHARD
> It's not like I remembered it.

> SAL
> It gets worse every time.

They turn into a bar (not the one at which Zeph and Sammy sat).

INT./EXT. BAR. NIGHT

The bar opens out on to a street just back from the beach. It is busy.

Sal and Richard stand at the bar with their drinks.

A hand rests on Richard's shoulder, gently pushing him aside to create space at the bar. It is Zeph.

> ZEPH
>
> Hey, it is Richard! How are you doing?

Sal watches the ensuing scene with cool interest.

Richard is at first friendly.

> RICHARD
>
> Hi.

> ZEPH
>
> Sammy! Come on over! Girls, I want you to meet The Man.

Sammy approaches through the throng at the bar with two young German women.

> SAMMY
>
> Hey, Ricardo!

RICHARD

Hi.

ZEPH

Hilda und Eva: diesem ist Richard – the man with the map. *Der Mensch mit den Wanderkarte.*

They acknowledge him.

SAMMY

They're coming to the beach with us, Richard. Sorry we haven't showed up yet. Just hanging out – you know how it is.

RICHARD

Hey, guys, listen, I got to tell you, I made a mistake.

ZEPH

A mistake? What mistake?

RICHARD

I mean, you know, there's no beach.

ZEPH

No beach?

RICHARD

Yeah. The map was a fake. It was like you said, the beach – it's just a myth. A story. That's all it is.

SAMMY

You went looking for it?

RICHARD

Yes. No. It doesn't exist. No island to get to. No beach to hang out on, nothing. The map, it was a . . . a mistake.

Zeph smiles.

ZEPH

Hey, come on, you wouldn't be holding out on us, would you? Let me guess: it is a fucking paradise?

RICHARD

No. Listen to me: it doesn't exist!

SAMMY

You know, Zeph, I think he's trying to put us off.

RICHARD

I'm trying to tell you to forget it, asshole!

The good mood has gone.

SAMMY

Well, that's the last time I offer you a beer.

Sammy turns away to Hilda and Eva.

He didn't used to be like this.

ZEPH

Man, you're all fucked up.

He too turns away.

Richard closes his eyes.

Sal puts a hand on his shoulder.

EXT. BUNGALOWS RECEPTION. NIGHT

Richard and Sal are sitting in the otherwise deserted dining area. The receptionist, Sumet, is at work in the background.

SAL

OK, so: you told them where you were going?

RICHARD

Yeah.

SAL

And they've seen the map?

RICHARD

Yeah.

SAL

Do they have a copy of it?

RICHARD

No!

SAL

We can relax a little: I doubt they actually have what it takes
to get there. But, Richard, I don't think we ought to tell
anyone else about this. It's just between you and me.

RICHARD

Thanks.

She stands up.

SAL

Don't mention it.

She walks across to the pool table where Sumet is waiting.

Sal produces the key for her room.

Now, I'm going to play a couple of games of pool with
Sumet. So why don't you –

She throws the key. He catches.

– go warm the bed?

Richard looks at the key in his hand then at Sal.

She smiles as she picks up a pool cue.

RICHARD
(*voice-over*)

Everything has its price, especially silence. I thought it over:
Françoise a long way off – no need for anyone to find out –
and of course, the thrill of something new. As prices go – this
one didn't seem too high.

INT. BUNGALOW. NIGHT

*The room is in darkness. Moonlight penetrates the threadbare curtain.
The bed is surrounded by a mosquito net.*

The music from the beach party is audible.

Just visible through the net is the outline of two human forms entwined.

EXT. BUNGALOW. NIGHT

Lizards scuttle across the small porch.

INT. BED. NIGHT

Surrounded by a wall of mosquito net, Richard and Sal lie on the bed.
Sal lies on her side, falling asleep. Richard is awake.

> RICHARD

Sal.

> SAL

Uh-huh.

> RICHARD

Can I ask a question?

> SAL

It was great.

> RICHARD

No, it's not that. I just wondered – about Bugs. And me.

Sal rouses herself.

> SAL

OK, it's like this. Bugs is my boyfriend, my partner, and you,
you're someone I just screwed. Is that OK?

She turns on to her side again.

> RICHARD

That's fine. That's absolutely fine.

> SAL

Good, now get some sleep – I may wish to have sex again
before we eat breakfast.

EXT. BEACH. DAY

Richard and Sal push the boat into the water and away from the beach,
jumping on board as they do so.

EXT. SEA/CLIFFS. DAY

Richard and Sal approach the outer cliffs of the sea-wall in the boat. Richard looks up.

Bugs is standing at the top of the cliff, directly above the cave.

INT. CAVE. DAY

The sacks of rice are now contained in a net being hauled upwards on a rope towards and into the chimney which rises out of the ceiling.

Sal swims away into the tunnel.

EXT. CLIFF TOP. DAY

Bugs and Keaty haul the rice up with the aid of a block and tackle.

INT. CAVE. DAY

Richard is alone as he looks up the chimney and watches the cargo disappear the last few feet to the top of the cliff.

As it reaches the top it is swung aside and Bugs looks down.

Richard and Bugs stare at each other down the length of the chimney.

Richard casually clutches his groin and thrusts once.

INT. LONGHOUSE/EXT. BEACH. NIGHT

The longhouse is full of inhabitants.

Richard walks the length of the hut dispensing the toiletries and other gifts. Unhygenix is particularly pleased with his gift – a pair of rubber gloves – and the randomly chosen sunglasses are well received.

He watches the people grasp at these items of civilized society.

Françoise is waiting for him in a relatively secluded corner of the longhouse. He gives her the camera.

> RICHARD
> For you. I know it's not as good as that one you left behind, and you may have to wait a while for the prints but –

FRANÇOISE

It doesn't matter. I like it.

He kisses her.

She breaks away.

RICHARD

What's wrong?

FRANÇOISE

How was it?

RICHARD

The rice run? No problem.

FRANÇOISE

No, I mean being with Sal.

RICHARD

It was fine. We got on OK.

FRANÇOISE

Some people say that she is attracted to you.

RICHARD

Really? Well, I would never have guessed.

FRANÇOISE

So nothing happened?

RICHARD

No. Of course not.

FRANÇOISE

You promise?

RICHARD
(*voice-over*)

I was so happy to be back, that I couldn't bear to spoil the moment.

(*on-screen*)

Yeah. Sure. I promise.

They kiss.

EXT. BEACH. DAY

All the inhabitants of the community, except Françoise, are standing together, facing in one direction.

> FRANÇOISE
> (*off-screen*)
> Closer together! That's better. OK. And smile.

Rapid montage of photographs taken with the disposable camera, showing the entire community, sub-groups within it, and various couples, ending with a shot of Richard and Françoise.

Close in on the last photograph.

> RICHARD
> (*voice-over*)
> So I started just where I left off. It was almost like our trip to Ko Pha Ngan never happened. Almost.

INT. LONGHOUSE. DAY

Richard is alone in the longhouse, lying on his bed, reading.

He hears the door open then close, and he looks up.

Bugs is standing at the door, staring at Richard.

> RICHARD
> Bugs. Hi.

Bugs says nothing. He scans the room. They are alone.

Richard senses unpleasantness ahead and slowly rises to his feet.

> Just you and me here, huh?

Bugs says nothing.

> You want to talk?

Bugs starts striding towards Richard.

> No, I guess you don't.

Bugs gains speed as he approaches. Richard readies himself then dodges Bugs at the last moment.

Bugs, cursing, pursues Richard around the longhouse, each of them trampling over possessions and partitions. Bugs is bigger, but Richard is too sly and nimble for him, taunting and mocking as he dodges around the narrow upright supports that run down the middle of the building.

Eventually Bugs catches Richard in a corner.

He grabs Richard by the throat and pushes him into the corner and up slightly, so that Richard is on the tips of his toes.

Richard is struggling to breathe and flails wildly but Bugs maintains the position, gripping Richard tightly at the throat and relishing his victim's suffering.

From outside a loud, horrified screaming begins.

It carries on and on.

Richard struggles to get a few words out.

Don't you think we ought to go see what the problem is?

Bugs pauses for a moment. He listens. The screams continue.

He drops Richard and turns his head towards the door.

Richard slugs Bugs on the jaw. A real haymaker.

EXT. CLEARING. DAY

Richard emerges from the longhouse rubbing the knuckles of his right hand.

A crowd has gathered as he joins it.

At the centre are Karl, on his knees, wailing and shouting in Swedish, and Sten, who has been savaged by a shark and looks dead. Despite his appearance, Keaty and Gregorio are attempting to resuscitate him.

> RICHARD
> (*voice-over*)
> Poor Karl: under stress, he didn't speak much English, but he only needed one word.

> KARL
> Shark! Shark!

Richard backs away as mouth-to-mouth and chest massage continue.

EXT. BEACH. DAY

Richard runs along the shore and begins to follow a bloodstained furrow in the sand.

Richard is standing over Christo who is lying in agony on the sand.

> CHRISTO
>
> Richard! My leg! My leg!

Richard looks at Christo's right leg; it has been badly savaged with long ragged tears in the muscle.

> RICHARD
>
> Yeah, your leg – it's – pretty bad.

Christo clings to him.

> CHRISTO
>
> But it will be OK? Please, Richard, when you bring the doctor?

> RICHARD
>
> The doctor?

CHRISTO

Tell me – it will be OK?

RICHARD

Yeah. Sure, Christo, it'll be OK.

INT. LONGHOUSE. NIGHT

Christo grimaces and screams.

He is lying on his bed, surrounded by various people, including Sal, Richard, Karl and Etienne, who is pouring alcohol/vinegar on to the wound and cleaning it quite vigorously with a cloth.

Etienne continues.

Christo is muttering in Swedish. As Sal speaks, Karl translates into Swedish.

SAL

Christo, we can take you to hospital, but you've got to remember that when you get there, you mustn't tell them where this happened. We have to keep our secret.

Christo replies in Swedish in between cries and grimaces.

KARL

He says we are to bring help here for him. He won't go on the boat. He won't go near the water.

SAL

Tell him that we can't bring anyone here. We can't do that.

Christo grabs Sal.

CHRISTO

Bring help! Bring help!

He falls back in agony.

SAL

We can't, Christo. You have to go or else stay here and take your chances.

Karl translates. Meanwhile, Sal turns to the others.

Anyone disagree?

No one does, although Etienne looks unhappy. He is about to intervene, when Christo starts shouting.

ETIENNE
What is he saying?

The word 'Sten' becomes clear.

KARL
He wants to know what happened to his friend.

EXT. GRAVE SITE. DAY

A freshly dug grave in a sandy soil about 1.5 metres deep.

The corpse (Sten) in a sleeping bag is slung into the grave, its feet protruding from the end.

Immediately, the earth starts to be filled in from either side.

Keaty is addressing the entire community beside the grave while earth is heaped on.

KEATY
We are gathered here today to pay our last respects to Sten.
He was a straightforward, reliable, friendly sort of guy who
worked hard and always made an effort to join in whatever
was going on. For example, he played cricket with an
enthusiasm that belied his Nordic origins, earning respect
with both bat and ball, and I think we can see that as
symbolic of his place amongst us in a wider sense. Anyway,
he wasn't one for long speeches, and neither am I. May God
take your soul, and you shall rest for ever in peace, mate.
We'll miss you.

Keaty holds back a tear as he throws a flower in the grave.

Others throw flowers in.

Bugs hammers a wooden cross into the ground behind the grave.

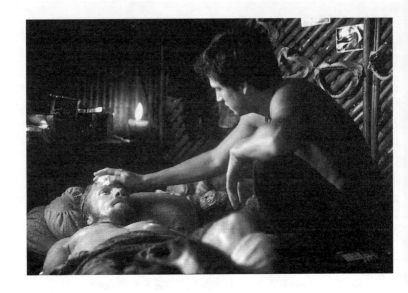

INT. LONGHOUSE. DAY

Christo is being nursed by Etienne who is mopping his brow, trying to get him to drink, etc.

Several people, including Sal, Karl and Gregorio, are sitting around, inactive and silent. A few attempt a game of cards with no enthusiasm.

Christo moans. A couple of people get up and leave.

> RICHARD
> (*voice-over*)
> After the funeral we all tried to get back to normal, but it just didn't seem right. After a while it became clear that the problem was Christo.

Christo moans.

People start to leave the building. Richard stays in place to observe.

> You see, in a shark attack, or any other major tragedy, I guess, the important thing is to get eaten and die, in which case there's a funeral and someone makes a speech and everyone says what a good guy you were. Or, get better, in which case everyone can forget about it.

Etienne turns to Richard.

> ETIENNE
>
> What do you think of all this?

> RICHARD
>
> It was a horrifying event, Etienne. A tragedy, for all of us.

> ETIENNE
>
> Yeah. But what do you really think?

He indicates Christo.

> RICHARD
>
> Really? I think I've seen what happens when a shark bites a man. I try, Etienne, believe me, I try, to get closer but that's it, that's as close as I can get.

Etienne returns to Christo.

> (*voice-over*)
>
> Get better or die; it's the hanging around in between that really pisses people off.

EXT. FOREST. DAY

Etienne is backing through the forest, outraged.

> ETIENNE
>
> This is disgusting! You cannot do this! Take him back!

A party of stretcher-bearers, including Bugs, Sal and Keaty, carry Christo through the forest. Richard walks behind.

> SAL
>
> OK, here we are.

They have arrived at a small tent that has been erected in the forest.

They lower Christo to the ground.

> ETIENNE
>
> Take him back, you fucking animals!

Sal drops the tent at Etienne's feet.

The party walks away.

Fucking bastards!

EXT. BEACH. DAY

People are playing and relaxing on the beach and in the water, shouting and swimming.

> RICHARD
> (*voice-over*)
> It would be a lot easier to condemn our behaviour if it hadn't been so effective, but out of sight really was out of mind. The bad smell was gone – it was like we had amputated Christo from our community and after the operation was over, we felt a whole lot better.

EXT. UNDERWATER. DAY

In water one metre deep, moving forward with a smooth side-to-side action, the POV of some underwater creature.

Small fish scatter ahead of it.

Suddenly a pair of legs come into view: they are Françoise's.

Close right in on them at speed.

EXT. SEA. DAY

Françoise screams as Richard surfaces beside her, laughing.

> RICHARD
> Just when you thought it was safe to go back in the water!

> FRANÇOISE
> That's not funny.

> RICHARD
> No, but it's certainly topical.

> FRANÇOISE
> Are you finished?

She turns away.

Françoise! I'm sorry. That was in bad taste. I don't know why
I said it. I won't say anything like that again. OK?

She still rejects him.

Hey, what's wrong with you?

FRANÇOISE
Your friend Sal is looking for you.

RICHARD
Really? Sal? What does she want?

FRANÇOISE
How would I know? But I'm sure it must be very, very
important.

EXT. BEACH. DAY

*Seen through binoculars, the beach on the other island (where Richard
and co. swam from). Zeph, Sammy, Hilda and Eva are there. Zeph
and Eva are studying a piece of paper (their copy of the map).*

EXT. HILLTOP. DAY

*At the highest point on the island Sal is looking across to the other beach
with binoculars. Richard is beside her.*

SAL
Now, Richard. Is that or is that not a map she's holding? And
did you or did you not make that copy?

Richard does not deny it.

You know, the lying doesn't bother me, but the map is
trouble. The farmers, you remember, the men with guns, they
told us: no more people. No more. And now it looks like
we're handing out fucking tour guides.

RICHARD
We could explain. Tell them about Daffy.

SAL
Explain? Who do you think we're dealing with? I want you up

here, every day, until they come. And then you get the map
back. Whatever happens, get the map.

Richard observes the lack of shade, water, etc.

RICHARD

Sal, they could sit there for weeks.

SAL

That's right. And you'll be here, waiting for them.

RICHARD

What am I actually supposed to do if they make the swim?

SAL

Get the map. You drew it, you gave it out, so now you get it
back, and turn them away.

RICHARD

But how?

SAL

You'll think of something. I have confidence in you.

Richard takes the binoculars.

Sal walks away.

Richard watches the other beach for a moment.

He turns to Sal who has already descended a few metres.

RICHARD

Sal!

Sal pauses.

SAL

You'll think of something.

She continues.

RICHARD

What are you going to tell everyone?

SAL

A story, Richard, and don't worry about Françoise, she'll
understand: she's in love with you.

EXT. HILLTOP. NIGHT

Richard is still keeping watch.

RICHARD
(*voice-over*)
This was truly a pain in the ass. I didn't want them to come to the island, but I didn't want to sit around waiting for them. I only hoped that Sal hadn't said anything to upset Françoise.

He hears a footstep behind him.

He turns and finds himself staring into a torch beam close up to his face.

Who is that? Sal, is that you? Will you get that light out of my eyes.

He is slapped across the face by a woman's hand.

Ouch!

FRANÇOISE
You pig!

She slaps him again.

RICHARD
Françoise! I'm sorry! I'm sorry! I'm sorry! Tomorrow – I'll spend all day with you! I promise!

Françoise pauses, still furious.

FRANÇOISE
It's not that.

RICHARD
It's not? Then what is it?

FRANÇOISE
You and Sal: on Ko Pha Ngan.

RICHARD
Oh, that.

FRANÇOISE
Yes, that!

She slaps him again.

She has told everyone. She has been telling people since the day you came back, and me, I am the last one to find out. At least she believes in honesty, not like you.

RICHARD
Come on, you were two-timing Etienne.

FRANÇOISE
Because I liked you. I didn't know you were going to fuck Sal the very next day.

RICHARD
Françoise, please, what can I say?

Françoise becomes calm.

FRANÇOISE
Nothing. There is nothing you can say.

She walks away.

RICHARD
(*voice-over*)
I was upset. Truly I was.

EXT. HILLTOP. DAY

Richard watches the other island. Zeph and co. are sunbathing inertly.

RICHARD
(*voice-over*)
For about twenty-four hours I was inconsolable. But grief, like love, tends to fade and be replaced by something more exciting.

EXT. HILL/FOREST. DAY

Richard crawls through the forest to an unseen destination.

RICHARD
(*voice-over*)
And life up on the hill turned out to be a big improvement. Up here, I could do whatever I wanted. There was no fishing

duty, no gardening shit, no hassle from Bugs or Etienne or Françoise.

EXT. FOREST NEAR DOPE FIELD. DAY

Richard is watching the dope Farmers from a safe distance.

> RICHARD
> (*voice-over*)
> And there were plenty of other things to keep me occupied.
> Apart from food I had no reason to go back.

EXT. CLEARING. NIGHT

The clearing is deserted, apart from Keaty.

Keaty looks around to make sure there is no one there as he backs towards the door of the small hut.

He signals to someone out of shot.

It is Richard on the edge of the clearing.

INT. SMALL HUT. NIGHT

Richard is sitting in a small, low, dark hut that is used for storage of tools and rice.

He is sitting cross-legged, barely visible, eating from a bowl of rice.

Opposite him is Keaty.

> KEATY
> Richard, what is all this? You sneak around, you don't see anyone, you don't talk to anyone. What is going on?

> RICHARD
> When I'm up there, Keaty, it's like I'm in a cross between Streetfighter 2 and every cruddy Vietnam movie you ever saw. I award myself three lives.

EXT. FOREST. DAY

Richard is sneaking through the forest from tree to tree, and crawling along a natural dip in the ground.

His movements are sudden and extreme at one moment, then he stands absolutely still at another.

In the lower left-hand corner of the screen are two small images of Richard.

Sound-effects of video game.

>   RICHARD
>   (*voice-over*)
> If I stand on a twig or disturb a bird or something, I lose a life.

He breaks a twig.

His main image fades for a moment and then is restored as one of those from the corner of the screen replaces it, leaving only one in the corner.

INT. SMALL HUT. NIGHT

Richard and Keaty continue.

>   KEATY
> What if you lose all three?

EXT. FOREST. DAY

Richard disturbs a few birds.

His images fade and die.

>   RICHARD
>   (*voice-over to Keaty*)
> Well, then I suffer great personal shame.

The words 'Game Over' flash on the screen.

INT. SMALL HUT. NIGHT

>   KEATY
> That's all?

>   RICHARD
> It's my game, OK? I can play to whatever rules I like.

III

                              KEATY
Of course you can, Richard.

                             RICHARD
Don't look at me like that, Keaty. I know it's just a game.

                              KEATY
Good, Richard, very good.

EXT. HILLTOP. DAY

Richard is on lookout.

                             RICHARD
                            (*voice-over*)
Keaty wasn't ready to hear the full details of my incursions.

EXT. FOREST. DAY

*Richard is sneaking around as before. But this time the four Farmers
are only a short distance away through the trees and Richard is still
edging closer.*

One of the Farmers is cooking chicken over an open fire.

Another steals a piece of chicken.

*The cook chases after the thief. The thief stops and turns, taunting the
cook with the stolen meat.*

*They fight a mock kick-boxing match, their moves pulled but swift and
practised.*

Richard watches, impressed.

*He picks up a stone and throws it into the forest beyond the Farmers. He
watches their sharp reaction to the sound, their moment of armed
alertness.*

The Farmers scan across the forest around them.

Richard stands absolutely frozen, sure to be seen if he moved.

                             RICHARD
                            (*voice-over*)
Sure, I knew it was just a game, but if you play the game with

enough conviction, it can take you a long way. With every day that passed I felt closer to my surroundings, closer to this island, until I merged with it, hidden, camouflaged, invisible.

The Farmers do not see him.

INT. SMALL HUT. DAY

Richard and Keaty meet again.

> KEATY
> Richard, why are you sitting in the dark?

> RICHARD
> To improve my night vision.

> KEATY
> And why would you want to do a thing like that?

> RICHARD
> I'm sorry, Keaty, that's classified.

> KEATY
> Classified. Right.

> RICHARD
> You know who I think about a lot?

> KEATY
> I have no idea. The Queen of Sheba?

> RICHARD
> Daffy.

> KEATY
> Daffy?

> RICHARD
> I admire him.

> KEATY
> You hardly knew him.

> RICHARD
> He had a certain style.

113

                              KEATY
Come here.

*Keaty beckons Richard to the wall where they peer through a gap to
watch other members of the community in discussion.*

They're talking about you.

EXT. CLEARING. DAY

                              SONJA
What does he do all day?

                           GUITARMAN
He doesn't go fishing any more.

                            GREGORIO
He doesn't work in the garden.

                              SONJA
But he steals our food, I'm sure of it.

                            GREGORIO
If he doesn't like us he ought to go home.

                              KARL
Idle, sponging, useless prick.

EXT. HILL. DAY

*From a vantage point on the hillside, Richard looks down on the
lagoon, the beach, the forest and the clearing.*

With the binoculars he can see the details of life in each of these areas.

EXT. ISLAND SCENES. DAY

*Through the binoculars: various characters are at work or at rest,
including Françoise, Sal, Bugs, Keaty, etc.*

                            RICHARD
                          (*voice-over*)
Maybe they didn't like me, but they still needed me. I was
outcast, observer, defender.

EXT. FOREST. DAY

The following five scenes are intercut.

On the trail through the forest, Richard is digging a hole about two feet deep, with his hands and a piece of wood, in the soft earth.

> RICHARD
> (*voice-over*)
> And if they didn't want to understand, that was their problem. I couldn't waste time trying to explain. I just had to be ready.

From beside the hole he lifts pieces of bamboo, broken and sharp at both ends. These he impales in the ground at the base of the hole, then he covers it with a skin of palm leaves. Over this he scatters some loose earth.

EXT. FOREST. DAY

Intercut:

Close-up: a caterpillar crawls along a green leaf.

Richard, his pupils dilated, is watching, transfixed.

He lets it crawl on to the tips of his fingers.

He sticks his tongue out and the caterpillar crawls on to it.

Richard gently closes his mouth.

He swallows.

EXT. FOREST. NIGHT

Intercut:

Richard is sitting cross-legged at a rough shelter composed of palm leaves and decaying logs.

A small campfire glows.

Between Richard and the fire is a small pile of mushrooms.

Richard lifts one and swallows it, then another.

(*voice-over*)

But when you're a highly trained combat-machine, you can't just sit around. You have to stay active. You have to put yourself in situations that will challenge you.

Staring into the fire he swallows a handful of mushrooms.

INT. HOTEL CORRIDOR. DAY

Intercut:

Richard is walking along the corridor in the Khao San Road towards Daffy's door.

Just as he is about to open it, the door is pulled open.

Daffy stands there in full combat fatigues, a 9mm pistol in his hand.

Immediately he checks that there is no one else in the corridor as he hauls Richard in.

DAFFY

Inside!

INT. DAFFY'S ROOM. DAY

The room is in a battle zone. The walls are pocked with bullet holes.

Daffy's armoury – Kalashnikov, sub-machine-gun, another pistol, hand grenades – is on display.

By one side of the window, a pair of military binoculars is mounted on a tripod directed out of the window.

DAFFY

Take a look, Richard!

Richard looks (intercut with moment of Richard on the hilltop lookout).

While Daffy loads and checks his weapons, and fires from the other side of the window, ranting aggressively, we see what Richard sees through the field glasses.

Snap cuts of:

– Zeph, Sammy and the German girls.

– The community in the clearing.

– Travellers on the Khao San Road.

Cancer, Richard, viruses! The big chunky charlie that's eating up the whole world! That's them, out on the street, down on the beach. Same deal: same disease. Pay them in dollars and fuck their daughters. Kicks off with four, then they multiply, Richard. Time to stop them, time to get rid of the human pollution. Year zero, kiddo!

RICHARD

Year zero?

DAFFY

You with me? Or against me?

RICHARD

I'm with you all the way, Daffy.

They pound knuckles.

EXT. FOREST. DAY

Richard is sitting at his shelter.

On his lap he has a lizard. He is gutting it and exposing the flesh.

He skewers a piece of meat on the end of the stolen knife and holds it out as though offering it to someone.

That someone is Sal. She is bored and declines the meat.

Richard shrugs and takes it himself.

SAL

Richard.

RICHARD

What?

SAL

Have you listened to a word that I've said?

RICHARD

I don't know: what did you say?

SAL

They're building a raft.

EXT. BEACH. DAY

Seen through binoculars, Zeph walks along the beach on the other island. He is carrying a large piece of driftwood.

He turns away from the water and walks up the beach towards the line of palm trees.

There he joins Sammy and the two German women who are in the early stages of constructing a raft from driftwood and polystyrene floats.

EXT. HILLTOP. DAY

Richard is watching through the binoculars, with Sal beside him.

SAL

I thought you were watching them.

RICHARD

Don't worry, Sal, it's not a problem; they won't get beyond the DMZ.

SAL

The what?

RICHARD

The demilitarized zone.

SAL

Call it whatever you like, Richard. Just stop them, OK? Bear in mind that this is an outstandingly bad time for anyone to arrive here: one corpse in the ground and another one still breathing in the forest.

RICHARD

Christo? He's still alive?

EXT. FOREST. NIGHT

In the small tent, a torch glows, outlining Etienne and the supine form of Christo.

Richard watches.

INT. SMALL TENT. NIGHT

Christo, delirious, is being nursed by Etienne.

Richard appears, crouching in the entrance of the tent.

> RICHARD
>
> So how's it going?

> ETIENNE
>
> What do you want?

> RICHARD
>
> Just checking up on the patient.

> ETIENNE
>
> Don't pretend you care; no one else does.

> RICHARD
>
> It's not that people don't care, Etienne, it's just that they don't care in the same way as you do. It's a fine distinction, I know.

> ETIENNE
>
> I understand: they wish he was dead.

> RICHARD
>
> No! They'd be equally happy if he recovered. They just want an outcome.

> ETIENNE
>
> He needs a doctor.

> RICHARD
>
> You worked in a hospital.

> ETIENNE
>
> For one month, as a cleaner, a domestic.

RICHARD

You know we have a sort of siege situation going on at the moment – obviously I can't discuss the details – but we all just have to adapt to the circumstances. And under these circumstances, you're giving him the best care he could possibly get.

ETIENNE

Look at this!

Etienne draws back the sheet covering Christo's discoloured leg.

Richard recoils from the smell and is then drawn back to the horror.

RICHARD

Jesus!

ETIENNE

It's gangrene. It's spreading. He needs an amputation.

Richard produces his knife (the stolen one).

RICHARD

Amputation? OK, so do it. Let's do it together, Etienne. My decision, your incision. Let's do it.

Richard slaps the knife into Etienne's hand.

Etienne is shocked.

I'll hold him.

Mesmerized, Etienne positions the knife. Richard puts one hand on Christo's leg and another on his chest.

Etienne grips the knife and holds it at the skin, poised to cut.

Richard can hardly contain his excitement.

Etienne drops the knife. He cannot do it.

Richard relaxes.

It's all right: I can imagine the rest.

RICHARD
(*voice-over*)
Curiously enough, Christo's sickness made me feel
invigorated, inspired even –

EXT. FOREST. DAWN

*On the upper part of the island, Richard ascends rapidly beside the
stream.*

RICHARD
(*voice-over*)
– as though by my proximity to his fading life I had tested the
condition of my own and found it stronger than ever. I was
almost ready for the climax of my game, the arrival of the
invaders. But there was no point in explaining that to
Etienne; in fact out of all the people I'd ever met, I knew
there was only one who would understand.

EXT. FOREST. NIGHT

Richard is seated as before at the small fire beside his rough shelter.

DAFFY
(*off-screen*)
Mushroom, Richard?

*Daffy is seated, mirror-image fashion, across the fire from Richard,
barely visible in the flickering light.*

RICHARD
No thank you, Daffy, I don't need any help to see the writing
on the wall.

DAFFY
I'm glad to hear that, Richard.

RICHARD
Got to keep my head clear.

DAFFY
It's getting close. Any day now.

RICHARD

Year zero, Daffy.

DAFFY

That's the spirit, kiddo.

RICHARD

You lead the way, Daffy, you showed me the truth.

DAFFY

But it doesn't matter what I think any more – it's up to you now.

RICHARD

And I won't let you down.

DAFF

You know what, Richard – no offence and all – but you're fucked in the head, right?

Across the flames, they shake hands.

EXT. FOREST. DAY/DAWN

Richard lies flat on the forest floor, the skin of his face and body disrupted by mud.

He smears on the last piece of mud.

He starts sneaking towards the rough shelter of wooden planks and palm leaves under which the four Farmers are sleeping.

INT./EXT. SHELTER. DAY/DAWN

The shelter is several metres long but shallow and is open down the length of one side.

This is the Farmers' home on the island.

It contains a collection of tools, arms, crates, bedding, food, cigarettes and bottles of cheap whisky.

Spaced out within the shelter, the four Farmers are asleep on low pallets or mats on the ground, each with their gun by their side.

Richard enters the shelter and surveys the scene.

He approaches the nearest Farmer who lies asleep. He is wearing a bandanna which has slipped half off in his sleep. His rifle and his knife lie beside him.

Very slowly, Richard reaches down and lifts the Farmer's gun, a Kalashnikov-type assault rifle.

Richard holds the weapon, becoming comfortable with it.

He lifts the butt to his shoulder and squints down the sight.

He closes in on the Farmer, so close that the muzzle is almost tickling the Farmer's nose.

In his sleep, the Farmer swats at his nose as he might swat at a fly. Richard withdraws the gun a fraction.

His finger strokes the trigger.

He moves very carefully around the shelter, pointing the gun at each sleeping Farmer and mouthing 'bang' as he goes.

He returns to the first Farmer and kneels beside him.

The Farmer is on his side, facing away from Richard. He stirs in his sleep and wakes slightly.

He reaches out behind him to feel for his gun. His hand feels the metal.
He relaxes and closes his eyes again.

Behind him, Richard smiles and releases his own grip on the gun.

Instead he lifts the knife.

He moves the knife towards the Farmer's head. He hooks it under the
bandanna and flicks it off.

He puts the bandanna over his own head.

He pulls the knot tight.

EXT. HILLTOP. DAWN

Richard stands at the highest point of the lookout.

He raises his arms in exultation in each direction: north, south, east and
west.

Finally, he faces the other island.

He raises the binoculars to his eyes and looks.

Slowly, he smiles.

RICHARD

At last.

EXT. BEACH. DAWN

Through binoculars:

Zeph, Sammy, Hilda and Eva launch their raft. It floats.

They climb on and begin paddling.

EXT. FOREST NEAR DOPE FIELD. DAY

Richard flits through the trees until he can see the shore.

EXT. BEACH. DAY

The travellers on their raft come ashore.

They consult their map then move into the forest.

EXT. FOREST NEAR DOPE FIELD. DAY

Richard watches them as they ascend the slope to the dope field.

In the other direction, hidden from the travellers' perspective, he notices the four Farmers sitting at their shelter eating breakfast.

EXT. FIELD. DAY

The travellers, watched by Richard, reach the top of the slope and then the edge of the field.

Zeph and Sammy wade into the dope. Hilda and Eva stand at the edge of the field, studying the map that Eva holds.

The Farmers are near by.

> RICHARD
> (*voice-over*)
> If I was going to warn them, then now was the time to do it.
> All I had to do was walk out and tell them not to make any
> noise, I could lead them to safety. I could persuade them to
> go. I could threaten them. If it came to the worst, I could lead
> them to the camp and we could kick the shit out of them,
> then send them home. But I didn't want to do any of these
> those things. I wanted to see what would happen.

The travellers are jubilant.

> SAMMY
> We are in dope heaven. There is no other explanation.

> ZEPH
> (*singing*)
> I smoke two joints in the morning, I smoke two joints at
> night, I smoke two joints in the afternoon and then I feel all
> right. I smoke two joints in time of peace and two in time of
> war. I smoke two joints before I smoke two joints and then –

Zeph stops singing. He has seen the Farmers, armed and watching him from a few metres away.

Sammy and the others also notice, one by one. They too stand still, dumb and frightened.

ZEPH

Hi.

SAMMY

Shit.

ZEPH

We're Americans. Tourists. But we will leave. We made a mistake. We go now. We take nothing.

Slowly, he begins to walk backwards, smiling reassuringly.

The Farmers say nothing but advance and outflank the travellers, herding them back into a huddle.

We go now. We leave in peace. Look we can pay. Here, American dollars. You can have them.

The Farmers line up opposite them.

All begin to plead desperately for their lives. The Farmers shout at them in Thai. It is not clear what they are supposed to do.

Here, take my watch. It plays a tune.

He presses a button and his watch plays a speedy electronic 'Star Spangled Banner'.

SAMMY

Mine too. And here, take these: real Ray-Bans.

ZEPH

And this torch. And this.

Zeph pulls out a knife.

The Farmer nearest him is startled and shoots. Zeph is hit in the chest, blown away, lifted off the ground and landing several feet behind the others.

For a moment, there is a horrified silence. The Senior Farmer curses the younger one. Then everyone, Thais and Westerners, realizes what must now happen.

The Farmers prepare to shoot.

Suddenly Eva breaks away and starts running, unwittingly, in the direction of Richard's hiding place.

One of the Farmers shoots at her repeatedly, missing.

The others start shooting at the remaining two, cutting them down in a hail of bullets.

Eva keeps on running, zigzagging as she goes.

The Farmers fire but miss.

She reaches the place where Richard is hiding, crouched down in the undergrowth.

Startled by seeing him, she stops abruptly.

Richard and Eva stare into each other's eyes for a moment.

Suddenly her chest explodes towards him as a single bullet rips through from her back.

She falls to the ground.

Richard is spattered with her blood.

He sits motionless for a long time, staring at her corpse.

Held in the fist of her outstretched right arm is the map. Richard sees it but does not move.

RICHARD

(*voice-over*)

So that was it. Now I knew exactly what would happen. I wouldn't need to wonder about it any longer.

Richard looks up. One of the Farmers is staring at him.

EXT. FOREST NEAR DOPE FIELD. DAY

Intercut with following scene.

Richard is fleeing in a state of panic.

He stumbles blindly through the thick undergrowth.

He pauses, lost for a moment, then starts again.

He changes direction. He looks back.

He sees the Farmer pursuing him.

EXT. FOREST NEAR DOPE FIELD. DAY

Intercut with previous scene.

The Farmer pursues Richard. He moves with greater confidence.

Eventually he catches sight of Richard.

EXT. FOREST NEAR DOPE FIELD. DAY

The Farmer pursues Richard who is fifty metres ahead.

Suddenly the Farmer falls, cursing and clutching one of his feet.

He has stumbled into one of Richard's man-traps, piercing his foot on a shard of bamboo.

Richard looks back for a moment then disappears.

EXT. UNDERWATER. DAY

In the pool at the base of the waterfall. It is empty.

Richard falls towards it, then submerges at speed from his jump.

He sinks then floats slowly towards the surface, eyes open.

(*voice-over*)

I tried to remember the person I used to be, but I couldn't do it – he got left behind in a hotel room in the Khao San Road along with the man who cut his wrists. And so long as I stayed here, I'd never find him again.

EXT. FOREST NEAR DOPE FIELD. DAY

Two of the Thai Farmers sling the body of Zeph into a hollow.

The third Farmer bandages his foot.

The Senior Farmer reloads the magazine of his automatic rifle.

EXT. CLEARING. NIGHT

Richard looks into the longhouse through a gap in the wall. The community is assembled for a party as Sal stands on a platform to speak.

INT. LONGHOUSE. NIGHT

Sal is at the centre of the longhouse, standing by the central pillar where the years are carved, delivering a speech to the assembled community who are in good spirits. A new carving, '0006', is in place below the others. Alcohol and cannabis have been consumed. The air is thick with smoke. Everyone holds cups of coconut alcohol.

Richard watches Sal speak.

SAL

I don't have very much to say. Let's start by admitting that we've had some problems recently, and accepting that we can all learn from those problems. But tonight I want to celebrate and I want to look ahead, because I see beyond any difficulties we might have had, I see that we have so much here to inspire us and to fill us with hope for the future. And I'm not just talking about this island, I'm talking about you. You make this place work, and it does. So let's hear it: to the island, to you, to the future.

They all cheer and drink, apart from Richard, who looks on in disgust.

Music starts, played on a personal stereo with speakers positioned beside the door.

Dancing begins.

Richard watches the party for a moment. His attention settles on Françoise.

She is joking with a group of people.

The smile vanishes from her face when her gaze meets Richard's.

EXT. CLEARING/FOREST. NIGHT

Richard pulls Françoise away from the longhouse and into the forest. She resists, struggling and calling loudly in a mixture of French and English.

> FRANÇOISE
Richard!

> RICHARD
Come on! We're leaving!

> FRANÇOISE
I'm not going anywhere!

> RICHARD
Shut up and keep moving!

> FRANÇOISE
Let me go! Let me go! Help! *etc.*

She breaks away from him and runs further into the forest.

Richard chases and catches her, bringing her heavily to the ground.

Françoise is shocked and frightened.

They both lie on the ground.

He relaxes his grip.

> RICHARD
What are you staring at?

Françoise remains silent.

Hey, don't worry. I won't hurt you. It's me. It's just me, Richard. You remember: the guy who can't play soccer. The guy without a girlfriend.

FRANÇOISE

I remember.

RICHARD

I've just been away, that's all.

FRANÇOISE

Richard – what happened?

EXT. FOREST. NIGHT./INT. SMALL TENT. NIGHT

The moribund face of Christo is surrounded by Françoise and Etienne, arguing in French, and Richard, who intervenes in English before.

ETIENNE

No!

FRANÇOISE

Listen to him, Etienne.

RICHARD

They killed four people. They'll kill anyone.

ETIENNE

I'm not leaving him.

FRANÇOISE

Please, Etienne, we have to go.

ETIENNE

You think I want to stay here? You think this is where I want to be?

Richard cuts in.

RICHARD

Look, Etienne, we're going, OK? Just the three of us. Like before, like nothing ever happened here. So there's nothing more to discuss. We're just going to go, right?

Etienne reverts to English.

ETIENNE

I'm not leaving him.

RICHARD

Then we'll take him with us!

Etienne laughs.

ETIENNE

Richard, look at him. Look at him. It's nearly over. You can't move him.

Richard thinks it through.

He and Etienne look at Christo.

They pause and look again at each other.

Etienne nods.

RICHARD

Wait for me at the boat.

ETIENNE

Be quick.

RICHARD

I will be.

EXT. BEACH. NIGHT

Françoise and Etienne flee through the forest towards the beach.

INT. SMALL TENT. NIGHT

Richard studies Christo, illuminated by a torch.

His breathing is laboured and irregular.

Richard tenderly washes Christo's face with water.

Richard bends forward and kisses Christo on the forehead.

He sits up and reaches out to Christo's face. He pinches his nose and covers his mouth.

Christo's body struggles briefly and goes still.

Richard relaxes his grip.

He covers up Christo's face and pauses in the silence.

He switches out the torch and crawls from the tent.

EXT. FOREST. NIGHT

Richard stands just outside the tent.

RICHARD
(*voice-over*)

I thought about the people at the party. I almost wanted to go back just to see Sal's face when the Thais walked in, but I thought: no, fuck it – I'm out of here.

In the darkness, very close, Richard hears a speedy electronic 'Star Spangled Banner'.

He turns towards it.

What!

Whack.

Richard is hit in the face by something heavy.

INT. LONGHOUSE. NIGHT

Richard awakes, lying on the floor.

It takes him some time (during the Senior Farmer's speech) to piece together what has happened.

One side of his head is matted with blood where he was struck.

Around and above him stand the community, all facing silently towards the centre of the room where the Senior Farmer is addressing them. He is wearing Zeph's watch on his wrist and a holster containing the revolver.

Behind him stand his three men with their AK-47s.

Etienne and Françoise are also present, frightened and subdued, several feet away.

Richard takes all this in and gets on his feet while the Senior Farmer speaks.

SENIOR FARMER

You think I want to hurt you? I am a farmer. That's all. You understand? I work. I send money to my family. If too many people come to this island, it's trouble for me: I can't work, I can't send money, my family don't eat. I said no more people, but more people come. So now you all go home. Forget this island. Forget about Thailand. You all understand?

He looks around. At first, no one says anything.

SAL

No.

SENIOR FARMER

What?

SAL

No. We will not leave. This is our home also. We built this house with our own hands, every last timber, and we will not leave.

Richard steps forward.

RICHARD

Sal, you're making a big mistake. If he says leave, then I think you ought to go –

134

SAL
Shut up, Richard: this is all your fault anyway.

Richard realizes that everyone is staring at him.

RICHARD
My fault? Fuck you, Sal.

SAL
Who copied the map, Richard?

Richard is silenced, sensing the accusing looks around him. The Senior Farmer approaches Richard.

SENIOR FARMER
You. You're the clever boy.

Suddenly he pulls Richard forward to his knees. He then draws his revolver and unloads all rounds but one as he speaks.

You're the boy who sneaks around, thinks we don't see, steals from us, plays with the guns. Yes?

He spins the chamber.

Richard nods.

And you bring people here?

Richard says nothing.

The Senior Farmer points the revolver at Richard's head.

I ask you: you bring people here?

Etienne steps forward.

ETIENNE
No! Let him go!

Etienne is knocked to the floor by one of the other Farmers.

RICHARD
Please, no, don't kill me – I didn't bring anyone.

The Senior Farmer pulls the trigger. No bullet.

SENIOR FARMER

Don't lie to me. You bring people here?

RICHARD

They were coming anyway! I tried to tell them not to!

The Senior Farmer pulls the trigger again. No bullet.

OK! Yes, I brought them, I copied the map!

SENIOR FARMER

And you watched what happened?

Richard looks up and into the Senior Farmer's eyes.

RICHARD

Yes. I watched.

They stare at each for a moment.

The Senior Farmer turns to Sal and holds out his revolver.

SENIOR FARMER

If you want to stay.

Sal is momentarily shocked. The Senior Farmer offers the gun again.

If you want to stay.

Sal takes the gun. She turns towards Richard.

Richard scrambles to his feet.

RICHARD

Sal! What the fuck are you doing? No! Don't be crazy, Sal!

She takes a step towards him. As she raises the gun, he backs away, seeking shelter beside people but they melt away from him in fear.

Sal! No!

SAL

You let us down, Richard. You brought us trouble.

Richard is suddenly gripped by Bugs who holds him tightly as Sal closes in.

Sal stands a few feet from him.

She trains the gun on his head.

Richard faces the gun. Sal is poised to pull the trigger now. She seems to hesitate.

BUGS

Do it. Do it.

The rest of the community is frozen, transfixed.

The Farmers look on with curiosity.

Sal's hand twitches.

Richard detects Sal's hesitation.

RICHARD

Come on, Sal, what's the big problem? All you've got to do is squeeze. Can't be that difficult, Sal. You know what the problem is? You can't do it, Sal, and you know why? Because if you pull that trigger – it's all over and you know it. Because it's not like Christo rotting out in the woods where no one sees, and not like the four people I saw shot today. This time everyone's got to watch, everyone's got to see what it takes to keep our little paradise a secret. Do it, Sal. Let them see the blood this time. See if they can take it.

They can take it.

She pulls the trigger.

There is no bullet.

Keeping the gun on Richard, Sal turns to the community.

They are backing away.

She turns back to Richard. She lowers the gun. Bugs, dismayed, relaxes his grip and Richard shrugs him off. Richard and Sal stare at each other.

EXT. SEA. DAY

Richard sits on the edge of the raft. Others sit behind him while several more swim close by or cling to the edge.

RICHARD
(*voice-over*)

But she was never going to leave. I don't blame her. Nothing back home was ever going to compare with what she had, and if you think you're in paradise, where else is there to go?

INT. LONGHOUSE. NIGHT

Everyone has gone, apart from Richard and Sal, and the Senior Farmer who waits in the shadows by the door.

RICHARD

Game over.

Sal nods.

SAL

Game over.

She lifts the revolver to her head.

She pulls the trigger.

EXT. SEA. DAY

There is a commotion on the raft and in the water.

Another boat is approaching.

It is a tourist cruise boat for day-trip tours around the marine park.

It draws alongside the raft.

People start climbing aboard from the raft and the water.

The deck is lined with tourists in a frenzy of photographing and videoing.

Richard remains on board, his back to the tourist boat, staring out to sea, towards the island.

RICHARD

The good news is that Françoise and I got back together and lived happily ever after. The bad news is that only happened on some other world, some happy parallel universe, the same where I didn't screw things up for everyone. But back on this one we just had to carry on living. For a while I tried to warn people to Be Careful, but no one listens and being careful – where did that ever get you? As for me, I've learned. What else can you do? So I tell people that I'm going to 'carry a lot of scars' for the rest of life. And it's true, I really am. But you know what the frightening thing is? That I like the sound of it, I actually like the sound of it: that I, Richard, am going to carry a lot of scars.

Twentieth Century Fox presents A Figment Film

CAST
(in order of appearance)

RICHARD	Leonardo DiCaprio
HUSTLER	Daniel York
HOTEL RECEPTIONIST	Patcharawan Patarakijjanon
FRANÇOISE	Virginie Ledoyen
ETIENNE	Guillaume Canet
DAFFY	Robert Carlyle
CLEANING WOMAN	Somboon Phutaroth
DETECTIVE	Weeratham (Norman) Wichairaksakul
TRAVEL AGENT	Jak Boon
ZEPH	Peter Youngblood Hills
SAMMY	Jerry Swindall
WOMAN WITH KEY	Krongthong Thampradith
SENIOR FARMER	Abhijati (Muek) Jusakul
FARMERS	Sanya (Gai) Cheunjit
	Kanueng (Nueng) Kenla
	Somchai Santitarangkul
	Kawee (Seng) Sirikanerat
	Somkuan (Kuan) Siroon
KEATY	Paterson Joseph
SONJA	Zelda Tinska
WEATHERGIRL	Victoria Smurfit
UNHYGENIX	Daniel Caltagirone
GREGORIO	Peter Gevisser
BUGS	Lars Arentz Hansen
SAL	Tilda Swinton
MIRJANA	Lidija Zovkic
GUITARMAN	Samuel Gough
CHRISTO	Staffan Kihlbom
KARL	Jukka Hiltunen
STEN	Magnus Lindgren
BEACH COMMUNITY MEMBERS	Myriam Acharki
	Andrew Carmichael, Josh Cole,
	Helene de Fougerolles,
	Bindu de Stoppani, Stacy Hart,
	Nina Jacques, Sheriden Jones,

	Gunilla Karlson, Sian Martin,
	Isabella Seibert, Elizabeth Thomas,
	Michael Thorpe, Timothy Webster,
	Ramon Woolfe
HILDA	Saskia Mulder
EVA	Simone Huber
SUMET	Raweeporn (Non) Srimonju

CREW

Directed by	Danny Boyle
Produced by	Andrew Macdonald
Screenplay by	John Hodge
Based on the book by	Alex Garland
Cinematography	Darius Khondji, ASC, AFC
Production Designer	Andrew McAlpine
Editor	Masahiro Hirakubo
Costume Designer	Rachael Fleming
Music by	Angelo Badalamenti
Co-Producer	Callum McDougall
Casting by	Gail Stevens
	Kate Dowd (Paris)
Unit Production Manager	Jo Burn
First Assistant Director	Nick Heckstall Smith
Production Supervisor	Santa Pestonji
Production Manager	Piya Pestonji
Casting (Thailand)	Raweeporn (Non) Srimonju
Location Managers	Phillip Roope
	Somchai Santitarangkul
Supervising Art Director	Rod McLean
Art Director	Kuladee Suchatanun
Set Decorator	Anna Pinnock
Property Master	David Balfour
Construction Manager	Ray Barrett
Horticulturist	Ross Palmer
Sound Recordist	Peter Lindsay
Special Effects Supervisor	Clive Beard
Stunt Co-ordinator	Marc Boyle
Script Supervisor	Anna Worley
Gaffer	Alex Scott
Digital Effects Supervisor	Robert Duncan
Digital Effects Producer	Drew Jones
Financial Controller	Bobbie Johnson

Chief Make-Up/Hairdresser	Sallie Jaye
Costume Supervisor	Steven Noble
Unit Publicist	Sarah Clark
Marine Co-ordinator	Lance Julian
Transport Co-ordinator	Arthur Dunne
Post Production Supervisor	Clare St John
First Assistant Film Editors	Neil Williams
	Paul Knight
Supervising Sound Editor/	
Sound Designer	Glenn Freemantle
Re-recording Mixers	Ray Merrin & Graham Daniel
Titles by	Tomato
Second Assistant Directors	Richard Styles
	George Walker
First Assistant Director (Thai)	Charlie Sungkawess
Third Assistant Directors	Andrea Slater
	Tippawan (Paew) Mamanee
	Usarawadee (Moo Dang) Eamsakul
Casting Assistants (U.K.)	Maureen Duff
	Will Davies
Casting Assistant (Thai)	Krongthong Thampradith
Location Manager	Michael Srisomsap
Senior Location Asistant	Lek Srisomsap
Location Assistant	Sujin Chumnina
Art Directors	Ben Scott
	Ricky Eyres
Assistant Art Director	Pippa Rawlinson
Assistant Set Decorator/Buyer	Phred Palmer
Props Buyer	Penjan (Pet) Buranasamut
Storyboard Artist	Jim Stanes
Scenic Artist	Oscar Wilson
Model Maker	Louis Glickman
Cartographer	Alex Garland
Art Department Assistant	Suttirat (Anne) Larlarb
Steadicam Operator	Peter Robertson
'B' Camera Operator /	
'A' Camera Focus Puller	Graham Hall
Focus Puller	Shaun Evans
Clapper/Loader	Ian Coffey
Key Grip	Gary Pocock
Grips	Jimmy Waters
	Phillip Murray

	Kittiwat (Jack) Hanprab
	Adun La-Ong-Orn
Camera Trainee	Andre Chemetoff
Camera Maintenance	Andrew Mossman
Video Playback Operator	Bob Bridges
Video Playback Assistants	Tid (Sun) Sarmsaeng
	Stuart Bridges
Boom Operator	Malcolm Rose
Sound Maintenance	Steve Finn
Second Assistant Editor	Denton Brown
Editing Trainee	Catriona Richardson
Production Co-ordinator	Judy Britten
Shipping Co-ordinator	Kanokporn (Keng) Sae Tang
Assistant Production Co-ordinators	Lulu Thorpe
	Porntipa (Geng) Phanbai-Ngam
	Daraphan (Aor) Sakornsathien
Assistant to Andrew Macdonald (UK)	Jenny Jones
Assistant to Andrew Macdonald and Danny Boyle (Thai)	Siriporn (Goi) Wongwatawat
Production Assistants	Virginia Murray
	Janpen (Jeab) Artayakul
	Veeranand (Kong) Vanijaka
Work Permit Officer	Pantipa (Ja) Thiemboonkit
Production Runners	Saipin (Omm) Kitsuban
	Singha (Eka) Yotha
Production Runner (UK)	Carey Berlin
Production Rushes Courier	Orapin (Tim) Chuenchom
Assistant Accountants	Kathy Ewings
	Claire Robertson
Accountant Assistant	Elaine Dawson
Thai Payroll Accountant	Panotte (Pong) Rattanajarn
Thai Assistant Accountants	Wannapa (Gai) Sinthunawa
	Chidchanok (Pam) Plodripu
Cashier	Caroline (Caro) Tapia-Ruano
Make-up Artist to Mr DiCaprio	Sian Grigg
Make-up Artist	Polly Earnshaw
Hairdressers	Tapio Salmi
	Barbara Taylor
Hair Colourist	Nicola Clarke
Assistant Make-Up Artists	Jutiporn (Ple) Aranyaputi
	Wattana (Keng) Garum
Assistant Hairdresser	Jeerapa (Aoy) Hasachai

Mr Joseph's Hair by	Glenda Clarke at The Beauty of the Nile
Costume Supervisor	Mutita (Air) Na Songkla
Costume Mistress	Natalie Ward
Costume Assistants	Kate Towns
	Supawan (Toi) Rodkird
Costume Cuter/Fitter	Panjaporn (Imm) Pearkpun
Costume Maker	Esme Young
Laundresses	Rachanok (Nok) Sup-Aree
	Pateeya Gunsrivieng
Costume Runner	Kowit (Bom) Wises
Senior SFX Technician	Steve Cullane
SFX Technicians	Kevin Rogan, John Fontana
	Ian Thompson, Wiroj (Roj) Nu
	Chalermpol (Pol) Pan
	Po Ketkorn, Prajuab Yasuk
SFX Administrator	Watcharachai (Samson) Panichsuk
SFX Labourers	Boonsong (Song) Neamsaad
	Chanin (Nin) Kitiwongsunti
	Sutin (Pom) Rakhan
Shark Design	Pennicott Payne Ltd
Senior Technician	David Payne
Technician	Anton Prickett
Greens Department Interpreter	Suriya Chaowanich
Island Greensman	Tiwa Punprasert
Props Supervisor	John Wells
Props Storeman	Gordon Fitzgerald
Supervising Standby Propman	Mickey Pugh
Standby Propman	Marlon Cole
Chargehand Dressing Propmen	Pol (Paul) Muangnum
	Somsak (Ood) Shuenchooluck
Dressing Propmen	Sanong (Nid-Noy) Chomtha
	Nipon (Ni) Hongsithipong
	Banchong Limtong
	Prapol (Nong) Sangsai
	Narongrit (Suea) Tangphoncharone
Props Department Interpreter	Jesada (Jest) Chitchaseon
Rigging Electricians	Stephen Pattenden
	Kris (A) Khanchanaphet
	Narong (Jom) Charoensuk
Armourer	John Nixon

Action Vehicle/Animal Co-ordinator	Thanadech (Ben) Thananorrakarn
Prosthetics Designer	Mark Coulier
Prosthetics Supervisor	Paul Spateri
Prosthetics Technicians	Duncan Jarman
	Matthew Smith
Foam Technician	Andrew Lee
Prosthetics Assistant	Simon Rose
Stunts	Jamie Edgell
	Eunice Huthart
	Gary Connery
	Joey Box
Stunt Co-ordinator (Thai)	Kawee (Seng) Sirikanerat
Stunt Performers	Pitak Janvijit
	Somjai Jonmoontee
	Natapong Plumchang
Stills Photographer	Peter Mountain
Publicity Services (Thailand)	Kith & Kin
Supervising Dialogue Editor	Max Hoskins
Assistant Sound Editor	Tom Sayers
Assistant Dialogue Editor	Susan French
Dialogue Editor	Nigel Mills
Sound Effects Editor	Peter Baldock
Foley Editor	Christopher Ackland
Assistant Music Editor	Hugo Adams
Foley Mixer	Kevin Tayler
ADR Mixers	Robert Farr
	Andy Thompson
Assistant Re-recording Mixers	Lyle Scott-Darling
	Adam Daniel
ADR Voice Casting	Louis Elman
Foley Artists	Paula Borham
	Stan Fiferman
	Jean Sheffield
Colour Timer	Yvan Lucas
	Mark Waddell
Laboratory contact	Paul Swann
Post Production Consultancy by	Steeple Post Production Services Ltd
Negative Cutter	Sylvia Wheeler Film Services Ltd
Gaffer (Thai)	Chesda (Pop) Smithsuth
Electricians	Robin Brigham
	Veera Sakronkun

	Sommat (Aud) Sangsinchai
	Charun (X) Srisumpun
	Arkom (Tom) Tangkhatok
	Sommbat (Jime) Tiyasuttiporn
Practical Electricians	Natta (Nat) Janyersiri
	Yothin (Yo) Jaiboon
Genny Operator	Panya (Bang Odd) Sangsuay
Rigging Electricians	Khanayutt (Yoi) Lhamlhe
Electrical Rigger	John Wright
Assistant Construction Manager	Kevin Harris
Construction Buyer	Jack Dyer
HOD Carpenter	Stephen Challenor
HOD Painter	David Meeking
Painter	John Davey
HOD Plasterer	Paul Tappin
HOD Rigger	Fred Crawford
Construction Co-ordinator	Vasu (A) Kantatham
Construction Foremen	Visit Sathirakorn
	Boontawee (Tor) Taweepasas
Assistant Construction Buyer	Kitiya Subpason
Standby Carpenter	Will Stickley
Standby Painter	Charles Cottrell
Standby Plasterer	Ray Roffe
Standby Rigger	Russell Prosser
Standby Stagehand	Peter Browne
Trainer	Cornel Chin
Voice Coaches	Vernice Klier
	Penny Dyer
Transport Captains	Woradet (Nui) Em-Eam
	Boriboon (Boon) Jarurongwatana
Transport Manager (UK)	Phil Allchin
Asistant Marine Co-ordinators	Hilary Julian
	Sharlan Julian
Marine Administrator	Bill Glesne
Dock/Barge Master	Michael Douglas
Marine Engineer	John C. Merrill
Zodiac Captains	Rhodes Barton
	Al Perry
	Douglas 'Kino' Valenzuala
	Danny Bailey
	Rob Wong
Marine Assistants	Chaiporn (James) Songmuang
	Preecha Songsakul

Mr DiCaprio's Security by	Galahad Protective Services
Medical Consultant	Dr Timothy Evans
Unit Doctor	Dr Nick Imm
Unit Nurse	Chantana (Pan) Pongrojth
Health & Safety Consultant	Cyril Gibbons
Safety Climber	Kevin West
Catering Supervisor	Chan Thananuntasiri
Craft Service Supervisor	Charn Chatpatumthong

Second Unit

Cameraman/Operator	Giles Nuttgens
Assistant Director	George Walker
Focus Puller	Brett Matthews
Clapper/Loader	Voranont Paipad
Script Supervisor	Zoe Morgan
Standby Propman	Gregor Telfer
Gaffers	David Smith
	Steve David

Underwater Unit

Director of Photography	Mike Valentine, B.S.C.
Focus Pullers	Robert Shacklady
	Gordon Segrove
Clapper/Loader	James Scott
Diving Supervisor/Camera Assistant	Christopher Goodwin
Video Assist/Playback	Peter Davey
Underwater Communications	Francoise Valentine
Safety Divers	Michael Thorpe
	Steve John
	Hadyn Thomas
	Teera Banditwong
	Boonmee Saisom
Production Assistant	Tom Pestonji

Aerial Units

Aerial Co-ordinator/Pilot	Marc Wolff
Aerial Camera Operator	Adam Dale
Aerial Safety Engineer	Tom Clode
Services supplied by	Flying Pictures Ltd
WESCAM provided by	WESCAM Incorporated
WESCAM Technician	Steven Winslow
Close Range Aerial Photography	Flying-Cam Inc.
Flying-Cam Pilot	David Storey
Flying-Cam Camera Operator	Louis Prezelin
Flying-Cam Assistant	Marc Asmode

Digital Visual Effects by
The Computer Film Company, London

Digital Effects Co-ordinator	Ruth Greenberg
Digital Effects Designers	Adrian De Wet
	Dan Glass
	Kat Szuminska
	Mark Nettleton
	John Thum
Head of 3D	Dominic Parker
3D Designers	Stephen Murphy, Justin Martin,
	Sally Goldberg, Richard Clarke,
	Chris Monks, Dayne Cowan
Digital Paint Artists	Siobhan Lo
	Alex Payman
	Ian Fellows
Digital Effects Editorial	Roz Lowrie
	Tabitha Dean
Digital Scanning and Recording	Jan Hogevold
	Steve Tizzard
	Adam Glasman
	Darrel Griffin
Additional Digital Effects by	Framestore
3D Design	Mike Milne
	David Marsh
	Daren Horley
	Richard Ducker
	Carlos Rosas
Video Compositing	Tim Osborne
Lighting Equipment supplied by	AFM Lighting Ltd
Additional Lighting Equipment	VS Services Ltd Partnership,
	Thailand
'LIBRA' Stabilised head by	Camera Revolution
Underwater Diving Facilities by	Mermaid Maritime Ltd
	Asian Adventures
International Travel	The Travel Company, London
Freight Services provided by	Renown Freight Ltd
	Trans Air Cargo Co., Ltd
Sound Transfers by	Synxspeed Post Production Ltd
Telecine Transfers by	Midnight Transfer
Post Production at	Salon, London
Post Production Sound	Reelsound Ltd
ADR recorded at	Goldcrest Post Production

	Facilities Ltd
Foley recorded at	Pinewood Studios
Opticals by	Cine Image, Peerless, Studio 51
Computer Graphics	Bionic Digital Ltd
Production Services In Thailand	Santa International Film Productions Co. Ltd
Orchestrations by	Angelo Badalamenti Patrick Russ
Score Conducted by	Phil Marshall
Additional Score and Remixing by	Barry Adamson
Score Electronics by	Phil Marshall
Music Editor	Gerard McCann
Orchestral Contractor	Isobel Griffiths
Music Preparations by	Dakota Music Service
Score Recorded and Mixed by	Geoff Foster
Score Recordists	Jake Jackson Ben Georgiades
Score Recorded and Mixed at	Air Studios and Angel Studios, London
Children's Choir	The Sylvia Young Theatre School
Choral Co-ordinator	Jenny O'Grady
Guitars	Clem Clempson
Percussion	Frank Ricotti
Keyboards	David Arch

SONGS

Snake Blood
Written by Neil Barnes and Paul Daley
Performed and Produced by Leftfield
Leftfield appears courtesy of
Sony Music Entertainment (UK) Ltd

Woozy
Written by Maxi Jazz, Rollo and Sister Bliss
Performed by Faithless
Produced by Rollo and Sister Bliss
Courtesy of London Records

Brutal
Written and Performed by New Order
Produced by Rollo & New Order
New Order appears courtesy of London Records

8 Ball
Written by Rick Smith and Karl Hyde
Performed by Underworld (Darren Emerson, Rick Smith
and Karl Hyde)
Courtesy of V2 Records/JBO Records

Beached
Written and Produced by Angelo Badalamenti
Remix and additional production by Orbital
Orbital appears courtesy of London Records

Porcelain
Written, Performed and Produced by Moby
Courtesy of V2 Records, Inc./Mute Records, Ltd. UK,
by arrangement with Warner Special Products

Spinning Away
Written and composed by Brian Eno and John Cale
Performed by Sugar Ray
Produced by David Kahne and Consulting Producer Brian Eno
Sugar Ray performs courtesy of Atlantic Recording Corporation

Pure Shores
Written by William Orbit, Shaznay Lewis and Suzanne Melvoin
Performed by All Saints
Produced by William Orbit
All Saints appear courtesy of London Records

Return of Django
Written by Lee Perry
Performed and Produced by Asian Dub Foundation
Asian Dub Foundation appears courtesy of London Records

Synasthesia
Performed by Junkie XL
Music and Lyrics by Tom Holkenborg
Courtesy of Roadrunner Records

Out of Control
Written by Thomas Rowlands, Edmund Simons and Bernard Sumner
Performed by The Chemical Brothers
Courtesy of Virgin Records Limited/Astralwerks

Fiesta Conga
Written by Patrick Prins and Ardy Beezemer
Performed by Movin' Melodies

Contains a sample of 'Somebody Else's Guy
(Me Did Love You')
Written by Jocelyn Brown and Annette Brown

Voices
Written by Stephen Spencer, Paul Geoffrey Spencer
and Scott Rosser
Performed by Dario G Featuring Vanessa Quinones
Courtesy of Warner Music U.K. Ltd/Reprise Records/Kinetic
By arrangement with Warner Special Products

Redemption Song
Written by Bob Marley

On Your Own
(Crouch End Broadway Mix and Walter Wall Mix)
Written by Albarn/Coxon/James/Rowntree
Performed by Blur
Courtesy of EMI Records Limited
by arrangement with Virgin Records America, Inc.

Bloody Boy
Written by Angelo Badalament and tom&andy
Courtesy of PolyGram Film Entertainment
& Lakeshore Entertainment

Neon Reprise
Written by Simon Schackleton and Howard Saunders
Performed by Lunatic Calm
Courtesy of Universal International Music, B.V. under
License from Universal Music Special Markets

Richard, It's Business as Usual
Written by Barry Adamson
Performed and Produced by Barry Adamson
Courtesy of Mute Records Ltd

Smoke Two Joints
Written by Chris Kay and Michael Kay

Yeke Yeke
(Hardfloor Mix)
Written and Performed by Mory Kante
Courtesy of FFRR Records/London Records 90 Limited
Under License From Universal Music Special Markets

Lonely Soul
Written by Richard Ashcroft, Wil Malone and J. Davis
Performed and Produced by UNKLE
Courtesy of M'Wax Recordings/A&M Records Ltd. London

Soundtrack available on London Records

Supaluck Tanthapichat
Sakda Sathirathai

Scenes from *Apocalypse Now* © 1982 Zoetrope
Studios,
All Rights Reserved.
Courtesy of American Zoetrope Film Library

There's Something About Mary
Courtesy of Twentieth Century Fox Film Corporation.
All Rights Reserved.

The Simpsons
Courtesy of Twentieth Century Fox Television.
All Rights Reserved.

The Producers wish to thank the following for their assistance

The people of Thailand, M. P. Thawat Wichaidit,
The Film Board of Thailand, Thailand's Royal Forestry Department,
Top Shop and Top Man, Dacor Corporation,
Boonrawd Brewery Co., Ltd. (Thailand), Luke Cresswell,
Junix Inocian, Bea Julakasiun

Colour and Prints by Technicolor Ltd.

Prints by Deluxe

Camera and Grip Equipment supplied by Arri Media

Originated on Motion Picture Film from Kodak

DOLBY® SR in Selected Theaters

Made in Thailand